JUST A Country Kid

Roy Goodwin

Grosvenor House
Publishing Limited

All rights reserved
Copyright © Roy Goodwin, 2021

The right of Roy Goodwin to be identified as the author of this
work has been asserted in accordance with Section 78
of the Copyright, Designs and Patents Act 1988

The book cover is copyright to Roy Goodwin

This book is published by
Grosvenor House Publishing Ltd
Link House
140 The Broadway, Tolworth, Surrey, KT6 7HT.
www.grosvenorhousepublishing.co.uk

This book is sold subject to the conditions that it shall not, by way of
trade or otherwise, be lent, resold, hired out or otherwise circulated
without the author's or publisher's prior consent in any form of binding or
cover other than that in which it is published and
without a similar condition including this condition being imposed
on the subsequent purchaser.

A CIP record for this book
is available from the British Library

ISBN 978-1-83975-528-6

Foreword

A few memories of growing up in the "Wilds" of Warwickshire at Eathorpe from 1936 till 1959

When I was known as Gudgeon by my friends

And thankfully we were allowed to be proper Country Kids

This is my way of thanking all of those I had the pleasure of growing up with,

I know some of the things I have written about are not in chronological order

But memories don't work like that, well, at least mine don't, so I hope you enjoy.

To Charlie

I hope you enjoy my tales of times long gone

Regards

Ray

The Preface

I was born on the 20th of January 1936 & supposedly took my first breath just as King George V took his last, Wow, what with this & "the Goodwin's" tenuous link with King Harold (Godwin) perhaps I've got "Blue Blood" in my veins. Erm, OK you are probably right, No I haven't.

I was named Roy after Harry Roy the band leader, Neville after someone my eldest sister Margaret fancied at school & Arthur after my Uncle, well three forenames, perhaps that shows the family had a sense of humour!

I was actually born in hospital at Rugby as Mum & Dad lived in a place at Grandborough that I have been told, shall we say "left a lot to be desired" so we moved to Eathorpe, which was closer to Royal Leamington Spa where Dad worked, so easier to get to work on a bike.

Obviously I can't remember anything for the first couple or three years & as this Tome is about my memories I think its best we forget that bit & get on with what are my genuine memories.

And of course like all good stories the best & only place to start is at -----------

The Beginning

As I turned the wheel the tyres screeched as I went round the bend, then the brakes squealed as I stopped my lorry. I had travelled so many miles today, as I did on most days. Sitting on the log box fixed to the brass fender in front of the black range in our kitchen, where there was always a kettle simmering. Mums old bread board was my steering wheel. The brass box with the Rexene cushion was, some days my car & some days my lorry, the rest belonged to my imagination. How I knew about squealing tyres or brakes I don't know because as far as I remember I had never been in a car. My folks never had one. Perhaps I heard something on the wireless which was only switched on occasionally. So it looks as if I learnt to drive at about four years old, though I bet there were times when Mum wished I hadn't, with the constant Brrrummmm Brrrummmmm & the tyres & brakes. I am sure that I am not alone in not remembering much until after I was about three. It was always lovely & warm sitting in front of that range & I can still taste that toast done on a twisted wire fork, with pork dripping with brown jelly spread over, YUM. But I never enjoyed the smell of dad's Herrings (when mum could get some) cooking on that thing hooked on the front of the grate YUK. I will always remember that deep step between our living room & kitchen a very deep step for little legs that at early times meant going down on my belly & up on hands & knees. Those red tiles on the floor could strike cold to the feet once you moved away from the range but were easy for Mum to mop.

As I think back over those times growing up in Eathorpe, it was perhaps the best place ever for a child to grow up, even in War-time, I don't remember much before the war. Tucked away in splendid green fields, woods and the shrubbery around the Park & the Hall. Where else could you wriggle through the fence at the bottom of the garden & there was the River Leam, with fish for young kids to catch. The river was also the place to see the otter hounds & huntsmen & women in their red or black coats, & their long poles that they sometimes used for prodding in the willow tree roots or rushes to scare the otter or to vault over the water sometimes falling In, sometimes to our amusement!. Later in life I was not disappointed when otter hunting was stopped, as even as a child I thought the otter, didn't stand much of a chance. I wonder how many people have been able to walk on a river bank & hear the otter pups mewing in the willow roots or rushes. It's an almost haunting sound that I never got tired of hearing. Alas like most rivers the Leam lost the Otters in the fifties, even though hunting had ceased.

Thank-fully the Water Rat (or Water Vole if you want to be accurate) could still be seen dashing along a "run" on the river bank or you could hear it munching the reeds or the "plop" as it went in the water if you were quiet enough. Kingfishers made a flash of colour as they dived from a branch into the water & emerged with a Stickleback or Minnow in their beak, then in the spring disappear into their nest holes, sometimes after the river had flooded a piece of bank would fall & a Kingfisher's nest would come into view with all the old fish bones. The sight of a Heron standing on the edge of the water perfectly still & then suddenly its head would go in the water like "greased lightning" & come back up again usually with a fish in its beak. Occasionally you could see a splash & a flurry in the water as a big Pike that had been lying in ambush in the rushes, grabbed a Roach, Bream or a Chub. Or even a Perch chasing a Minnow or Stickleback. The Moorhen or Coot busily bobbing their heads as they swam & dived, looking for food, also the distinctive "plop" of a Moorhen chick learning to dive. I suppose we nearly had our own zoo or aquarium right on our doorstep except our animals & fish were free.

WWll

A vivid memory has stuck in my head all my life & I suppose the first real memory of something outside our house, of a November night in 1940. Standing outside our back door, Dad in his Sports Jacket & his trousers held up with an old tie & a shirt with a loose collar & tie, this is what he always wore every day summer or winter, mum with a coat over her, (don't know whether you call a pinafore or an overall but she always wore it to keep her frock clean, we just called "a pinny"), & me in my red coat with a black collar, I bet I looked good in that. Feeling cold & trembling, seeing the flashes & seeing the glow in the sky of the buildings on fire. Hearing the bombs exploding on Coventry & listening to the planes over-head with guns firing at them. Seeing the Search- lights scanning the sky & pinpointing some planes. Like millions of others we heard the expression "is it one of ours or one of theirs". We soon learnt the different sounds, the heavy German bombers & the Fighter Planes sounding sharper. As a child of four perhaps the trembling was not just cold, I suppose it was exciting, being much too young to realise that people were dying, I'm sure that I obviously didn't know what it was all about & certainly didn't know it would be five years before it would end.

Living in a small Hamlet, we thankfully missed all the horrors that people in towns & cities endured. We still had to have Blackout Curtains & brown sticky tape crosses on all the windows in case of a blast. We heard reports of the devastation of towns on the wireless, which was a mains set so that meant

Mum or Dad didn't have to go to Wappenbury to get the accumulator charged at the garage, like a lot of people. Nearly every house in Eathorpe had electricity fitted but there were some in the Village (it's a Hamlet really) & around the outlying farms that relied on Paraffin for light & most houses had a Paraffin stove of some sort to warm those cold corners when you couldn't get coal. I think only the Park, The Hall & Reeve's had running water by electric pump, everyone else had to go to their nearest pump, which meant you didn't waste water! The pump we used was behind our row of houses & was shared by six houses, there being a footpath between our backyard & the garden, the water was crystal clear & had a sort of sweet taste coming out of the pump stone cold. In the winter the pump was covered in straw to stop it freezing & then an old bit of canvas wrapped round to keep the straw dry, but when you needed water you had to take the canvas off. Remembering taste reminds me of having a spoonful of Cod Liver Oil & Malt every morning for vitamins, & when you moaned about the taste you were told"it's not meant to taste good, it's meant to do you good" just like Medicine.

Our Toilet or Lavatory as most people called them then, was in a building that was also the coal shed, attached to the kitchen, which meant at least, we didn't have to go to the bottom of the garden like most & we had an electric light in there which meant we didn't need a torch to see the spiders. Though you still had to go outside. There was a board with a hole & a large bucket below behind a door. Which had to be emptied in the garden when full (great for the vegetables), there were squares of newspaper on a nail (never use the Woman's Weekly much too shiny). After the war the Council provided "Night Soil Men" (we had a different name for them but I wouldn't repeat it here) who came round with a lorry every week & emptied the buckets (not the best job in the world.) The garden was still quite often used!! The buckets were large galvanized ones with a big handle & one of the

Night Soil Men was so short he really struggled to keep the bucket off the ground, but he did the job for years & guess what he was called Shorty! & was one of Doreen's uncles from Leamington, Oops forgot the Royal & Spa bit. Under every bed was a Poe, Chamber Pot or Guzunder whatever you called it, they were quite big white china things that Mum used to empty into a white enamel bucket every morning hoping that no-one had been really "took short" in the night.

Bath night was usually Friday when the copper in the corner of the kitchen would be filled with about three buckets of water & wood was brought in from the shed & lit. The tin bath was taken off the hook in the back yard & placed on the kitchen floor & the Carbolic or sometime Palmolive soap got out then it was time to take turns, with the bath being topped up with hot water It didn't take too long if Nina & Margaret were at Rugby because there was only me & mum (unless we had people staying). I can never remember Dad ever having a bath, he preferred just to have a strip wash! He shaved every day & nearly always cut himself, so he was regularly seen with a bit of newspaper stuck to his chin! Even though he always used a "safety razor"!

You always called adults by their surnames like Mr or Mrs Timms unless they were neighbours then they became "Uncle or Aunty!" I even had "Uncles & Aunties" by my Grans at Rugby some half a street away.

Dad worked at The Lockheed Company in Leamington Spa where he was a foreman Electrician & Key Man whatever that meant (learning his trade around Rugby when big houses had generators & was happy to tell of his adventures with servants), cycling to work in all weathers & sometimes weird times. I liked the Lockheed because just before Christmas us kids were treated to a party with a Pantomime & I was able to tell the others my dad made Santa's Sleigh that used to travel over the stage. I remember one year at the party my present from Santa was a Morse Code Set, which meant I became a Captain of a Ship sending messages round the world (usually SOS) which made a change from driving my lorry. The Christmas Parties were held on a Saturday afternoon so it meant I could go because there was a bus but I had to make sure I left in time to catch the bus home because there was only one.

Cycling to work meant you had to have lights on your bike & batteries were always difficult to come by. Dad was either putting his batteries from his lights by the fire to "resurrect" or moaning that his dynamo was slipping on the wet tyres & unless you were doing a decent speed you could have got more light from a candle. Some people still used Carbide lamps but Dad never had one, but those who did always had somewhere to warm their hands. They were a marvellous bit of kit, though expensive (that's why dad didn't have one). You put some carbide rocks in the bottom of the lamp, you put water in the container over the rocks, then you set the tap to allow a drop of water onto the carbide this made acetylene, which you lit & it gave a white light. (Whilst carbide was readily available the older lads taught us perhaps the most stupid & dangerous thing we ever did, fishing with carbide. You put a very small rock of carbide in a pop bottle put in some water screwed the top on tight then threw it in the water quick. The bottle exploded & the stunned fish came to the surface but it was never done where we would go bathing because of the glass. How none of us ever got hurt was next door to a miracle) Dad always had a couple of table spoons & a puncture kit in his pocket! He became very skilled at doing a repair in the dark, for either a puncture or a broken chain. Dad's bikes had all seen better days! During that time you were only allowed a small light so even bike lights needed to be part covered. Towards the end of the war German POWs from Birdingbury Camp used to walk to Eathorpe (about four or five miles) &

play football with us kids, in Brian's field & they played barefoot. We had great times, they didn't run rings round us but I know they could. (These were the same men we saw digging drainage trenches in the marsh. They had a uniform with a big coloured disc on it, the Germans & Italians had different colours & shapes).

There was nearly always a pot of tea with a Cosy on, either on the side of the kitchen range or on the hearth in the living room, but as tea was short quite often the old leaves would be left in & a few fresh leaves added when a "new" pot was made, making sure of course it had time to brew as you didn't want any floaters! But she always made a fresh pot when Dad got home from work or if some-one came who she wanted to impress, even the best china & the tea-strainer, would come out then. No teabags then just loose tea leaves, when you could get them. The used leaves were spread on the garden because Dad said they were good for his Pansies & Snow on the Mountain. When sugar was short Mum (who didn't take sugar anyway) tried to use saccharin, Oh dear that didn't go down well with Dad. Instant Coffee was in a bottle that had something to do with Chicory & made by Camp I think, there were other cheaper ones but even for a kid who would eat & drink almost anything some were awful, but people didn't drink so much coffee then, other than posh folks with Percolators. One of the few delights I had as there were virtually no sweets to be had was, when the Rhubarb that grew in a clump at the bottom of the garden & had been well fed with manure (not the human sort) & was covered with an old small bath tub that had a hole in the bottom, was ready to eat a stick would be pulled, the root bit & the leaves (which I think are poisonous) were cut off, a spoon full of sugar (when Mum had some) was put in a piece of paper & you dipped the Rhubarb in it & bit a chunk off, Cor that was delicious. Another treat was, to unwrap an OXO cube & nibble till it was gone & if there was a tin of Condensed Milk in the pantry having a Condensed Milk sandwich, we are now told that that sort of thing is bad for you but then it was something special. Usually in sandwiches we had meat paste out of a little jar which was OK & sometimes I had the chance of running my finger round inside the pot to get the last bit out, then lick your finger but fish paste I just could not get to like, but Mum & Dad loved it so that meant we had it & I ate it. Because it was no good saying "I don't like that" if you didn't eat it there was no alternative (No use being "a fussy eater" then). Why is it that everything we enjoyed as a kids, is now supposed to be bad for you? Like chips cooked in beef dripping, pork dripping sandwiches, carrots pulled from the ground & eaten without washing & of course full cream milk straight from the cow. How did we survive?

Evacuees

We heard many things from the people who were coming into Eathorpe, every night from Coventry & staying in our houses overnight to escape the bombs. We had some evacuee children from London but only one called George who came from Rotherhithe stayed (he stayed with Mr & Mrs Timms the coal merchant). Julie & Eric's family also were evacuated to Eathorpe from Coventry. The nearest we got to bombs was when dummy factories were built in the woods not far from Eathorpe & set alight, to try and draw the bombs from the Factories in Coventry by making it appear there were factories alight, which must have been really scary for the people living in the farm houses at either end of the woods.

Mostly Incendiary bombs, were dropped on them & my sisters Margaret & Nina used to go with others & collect the empty cases, when they were at home from Rugby. Which Dad got Chrome Plated at work at the Lockheed, to be kept as ornaments? There were also at least two bombs dropped either in error or if a German plane had to dump one, these made holes in fields one not too far from Hunningham but no-one was hurt & no damage done.

I well remember one couple who stayed with us from Humber Road Coventry, (the husband worked at the Humber Car factory & his wife was a very small timid lady), who every night brought with them in their big black car a Pekinese dog & a Parrot, neither appeared to like little boys. The dog used to snuffle & yap at me but the Parrot would attack anything in sight, particularly fingers. (It took me quite a while to realise not to get too close to the thing, I should have known better as Gran had one as well, slow learner!) Perhaps that's why I have never had an inclination to have a Parrot! I do remember going to their house after the war (it obviously survived the bombs) & it was quite big & very posh compared with ours.

Now I think back we always seemed to have people living at our house & I don't know how it was done because it was not that big. A kitchen & a sitting room, a hall, two double bed rooms & a very small single, but we seemed to manage. By now my brother Bob who had been a very good rugby player, playing for Warwickshire School Boys at an early age as full back (I was too young to see him play actually I don't think I was born) & had worked in Jimmy Malin's yard in Railway Terrace (Jimmy was always known as a bit of a "Jack the Lad" & always "ducking & diving" even offering to take on Houdini in an escape trick & had always got some gadget to flog & I'm sure Bob tried to keep up with him), learning how to make anything work if it had an engine in it, was in the army. After being brought up by my Gran-parents in Rugby (No, I never did find out why, nor why Nina & Margaret went to school in Rugby either). In 1940\41 Bob got married while on leave (I think it was demarcation leave) to a really nice girl from Rugby called Edith but didn't come home again until after the war. My two sisters were quite a bit older than me Margaret was thirteen years older & Nina was ten years older (I suppose I was an after-thought or perhaps one too many pints) They were working in Rugby on the buses or in the Portland Cement Offices, & were living with Gran. While in the army Bob was in the Glosters & the Tank Regiment still plying his trade at making things work but not just cars, motorbike or trucks but mainly tanks.

Mum really was not a very good cook, but there was always something served up. Dad always said she could spoil boiling water (but I survived) & I can never ever remember Dad cooking a meal or even making a cup of tea. Mum's needlework (she trained as a seamstress) was always a family joke, if you had a button come off it was stitched back on with whatever colour cotton was in the needle & the chances of it staying on were not good "red hot needle & scorched thread" was the expression, her darning was a real joke! The thing that always amazed me was no matter how much "her leg was pulled" about things she just smiled. But it does mean I can cook & stitch a button on or if needs be get the sewing machine out.

The only time I can remember going into a Café was to a WRVS canteen (café) on Regent Grove in Royal Leamington Spa, when they sent me out of hospital for being sick & there as a long wait for the bus, we had Dried Egg scrambled I think on toast & a cup of tea, Cor we knew how to live.

Rugby

Grandad Walker died about this time after spending a long time in Hospital. My only real memory of him was, seeing him on Hillmorton Road struggling along on two sticks when he had been allowed out of Hospital for a walk, shortly before dying of Bowel Cancer. Gran-dad (he was known as Hooky but I don't know why) had always worked on the railway as a tuber, (I think), so they lived in a row of Railway Houses on Newbold Road, which were fixed to the main-line bridge & also opposite the Gas works. Gran never needed a clock, she could tell the time by which train went by and the ornaments on the mantle-shelf would rattle with the vibration. The smell & the noise of the waggons being shunted from the Gas Works was something that took a lot of getting used to. If I was at Gran's I would go with Uncle Bill, to collect coke from the gas works in a wheelbarrow, for the fire, when she was getting short of the coal, the Railway Company L M S still provided even though Grandad had died. Behind the houses was a green with houses on three sides & the railway signal box & a main line on the other. There were a load of Anderson Air raid shelters that were used as play areas for the local kids, I don't know if they were ever used in an air raid. There was also a little general store that even opened for two hours on a Sunday! & a cobblers run by Albert Prestige "Preckit" who wore a surgical boot with a sole about two inches thick. This was where the local kids used to congregate. I don't know whether it was the smell of the leather or the ammonia he put on the soles to make them shine, the rattle of his sewing machine or the whine of the electric Buffer or even the folding ruler that we loved to play with even, though we were told he would wring our necks if we broke it, but there was something magical about that wooden shop. It also meant that if I had a hole in my shoe & I was at Gran's she would pay to have it repaired & Preckit would find time & leather to do it! She would say "go & see Preckit & say Mrs Walker sent you" (good old Gran). If you were at Gran's on a Sunday in the summer, occasionally she would insist that we went up to the Park to listen to the Band in the Bandstand. One of my first memories of being at Grans was standing talking to another boy in her bedroom or at least I thought I was! I was actually standing in front of a full length, mirror on the wardrobe, we never had one of those at home!

How everyone fitted into Grans house I don't know downstairs there was a front room that was only used at Christmas in which was a sofa & chairs, stuffed birds in a glass cabinet & an old Harmonium (that I spent hours peddling & making an almighty row on) & for a while a green Parrot, that didn't like little boys just like the one from Coventry (perhaps it was just me) never did know what happened to that, the living room that had a table & chairs, Grans chair was an old bus seat, (I expect Bob got that from Jimmy Malin's scrap yard), a radio gram that belonged to uncle Arthur, & Gran always listened to the news & Sunday Half Hour on (woe betide anyone who spoke during either) a kitchen with a sink with hot running water, a bath with a wooden cover on at the end with a gas Geyser over (I never saw the cover off that bath but I suppose it must have been used) out-side there was a small yard with a FLUSH toilet, perhaps two of the enjoyable things about going to Gran's was to play with her Kaleidoscope & hear the water flush. As she only had two bedrooms with one part curtained off at the top of the stairs. My uncle Bill who was the local chimney sweep, was still at home but he slept in Gran's room because he had fits (which he eventually died of). My uncle Arthur who had worked in the offices of Willens, was also in the army in Gibraltar after being "called up" but alas when Gran-dad died & because he was not allowed compassionate leave to attend his funeral, he decided to join his dad & shot himself. (So sad I never got to know him & I have since seen a picture of his grave in the Military Cemetery in Gibraltar).

Gran had two soldiers billeted with her, I think they were guarding some of the Electric Companies or the railway as Rugby was a major depot. My sister Nina married one of those soldiers Jack & Margaret was courting farmer's son Joe from Wappenbury who she later married. Visiting Gran was always an adventure, as we had to walk to Princethorpe to catch a bus, a long walk for little legs (& older legs) or an even longer walk to Marton Railway station to catch the train & another long walk from either the Bus Station or the Railway station (they were opposite each other by the Cattle-market) along Wood Street to Newbold Road. I only knew my mum's parents, as there had been a big fall-out when Mum & Dad got married but I did meet dad's dad, Gran-dad Goodwin when I was sixteen but (that's another story) I don't know whether dad was too old for the forces as he served in WW1, in the Royal Flying Corps or whether it was his Key Worker job at The Lookheed, but he joined the AFS (Auxiliary Fire Service) which meant every so often they would play with a pump by the river, I don't think they ever saw a real fire!!!! I must have been nine when Gran died & not long before then Mum & I visited one of Mums old friends from Grandborough (where Mum Dad lived in an awful Tin & Wooden house where they said the rats even ate the soap, before moving to Eathorpe), Mrs Gee, who lived at Lawford (not sure whether it was Long or Church). It meant a bus to Rugby then another to Lawford, the Gees lived opposite an Airfield that was a bomber station. Now whether we went because it was an "Open Day" or whether it was a coincidence I don't know but it was magical looking round those Aeroplanes (which means it must have been after 1945), even if it was for a short time, as we had to catch the bus back to Rugby. Just as we were leaving Mr Gee came home from work. He worked on a road gang with a tar sprayer, loose chippings & a steam roller, his boots were solid with tar & I bet his trousers stood up on their own. There is something about the smell of tar. We had to spend the night at Grans, as there was no way to get home that night.

Oh those games we played

Being that much younger than my brother & sisters meant I didn't have siblings to play with, but in Eathorpe we were allowed to go out to play when we were four or five, because we could, as there was very little traffic. We had a Hop Scotch square marked out in the road, & a skipping rope (some-ones Mum's clothes line or on old plough line) would be used across or along the street. The girls were brilliant at skipping & sometimes would use two ropes, I just about managed one provided it was not too quick! Marbles was always a good game particularly if you could get a big ball bearing that would be King. Trying to pull up the drain in the, road when a marble went in was a bit of fun, because you never knew what else you would find.

There was about twelve of us kids about the same age living in the street & around. There was David, Percy(Choggy), Gwen, Brenda (Snowy) Eric, Julie, George (the evacuees) Oonagh, Shirley, Jack, Jill, Doreen, Pauline (who had a younger brother Robin, who had a moment of fame when he was taken to hospital after being badly stung in his nether regions through poking a stick in a Wasp Nest) & me. What a great lot of troopers we were! There were others older & younger but they didn't join in our games Though I well remember playing by a hay rick not far from The Plough pub with some of the older ones when I was seven or eight & I suppose you could call it my first sex lesson! I certainly enjoyed playing "Post-Mans Knock many times afterwards. I wonder if kids still play Sardines, Hide & Seek, Postman's knock, Mums & Dads,

Doctors & Nurses. Of course who could climb the highest up a tree was a must. We all had our favourite tree, mine was a big Copper Beech where I built a bit of a platform, where I would only show my best friend at the time how it get to it. We made wonderful dens, that you only allowed your friends (of that day!) to enter. Most of our games were in the shrubbery that lined the drives of The Park & the Hall & also the wide Privet hedge round Reeves's garden that was hollow in the middle. It was during some of these games that we really learnt the difference between boys & girls, & I am sure that stood us in good stead for later life, or at least did us no harm. (When George's slightly older sister came for a holiday from London, she certainly taught us things we didn't know! & we certainly enjoyed learning them behind a blackberry bush)

I wonder how many kids now get a chance to know how, to make a boat that floats from a reed & a thorn from the Blackthorn, how to make a brilliant peashooter from a piece of Elder wood, using a meat skewer to remove the pith out of the middle, or a piece of Keck from the roadside making sure you were careful with the hairs on the outside, as they could give you a rash (the penknife was good for scraping them off) & using Elder Berries instead of Peas If you couldn't find any dried ones in Mum's Pantry, to make a "tank" out of a cotton reel (sometimes with the cotton still on) an elastic band, a apiece of a candle & two matches, we used to race our "tanks" & some-times make little grips in the rims of the reels so they would climb the edge of a home-made Peg Rug. Or who could make a banger from two bolts, one nut & the top of a match. How many kids now know when to eat Pig Pears, Crab Apples, Walnuts from under the tree, (I got into trouble at school after picking up walnuts too soon and getting very yellow hands from the outer shell, I think they thought I had been smoking heavy!) or wild Hazel Nuts without being very sick & if you have ever been sick through eating too many unripe Crab Apples, or Gooseberries you will certainly know what I mean. We did, though, sometimes we got it wrong & were very sick (clip round the ear time). You learnt which leaves to eat (new Hawthorn leaves taste like bread & cheese & Sorrel tastes like Vinegar) & rub Dock leaves on legs & arms after being stung by nettles or most other things, but you ran home for The Blue Bag if it was a wasp or bee! We regularly walked across the fields to the woods where the dummy factories were built & had great adventures finding Rabbit, Fox & Badger holes & us lads bragging what we would do if we saw one of the occupants (knowing full well we would do nothing), or collecting a bunch of Violets or Primroses for Mothering Sunday (I think that could be called bribing Mum). We also went to The Marsh to collect Lady Smocks, King Cups or Peewit's & Snipes eggs knowing that all ground nesting birds run from their nest before taking flight, so it was no use just looking where the bird took off. Then getting into real trouble for getting covered in mud from head to toe. We made catapults from hazel wood fork & strips of inner-tube & a bit of leather from an old belts, that we spent hours practising with, hoping one day to hit our target. On Saturdays & during holidays in the Fox hunting season we would make our way to the Gated Road, if the hunt was meeting at the Hunningham Pub. Just in case they came towards Penteloes, arguing which gate to have, we then would open the gate & sometimes get sixpence. Scrumping apples from Flannel Reeves orchard (of course he knew we did it & didn't seem to mind) & Cobb nuts from the plantation at the Park (the owner of which, if he saw you, would fire his shot gun over your heads, that's when you learnt to run) The Eathorpe Allotments were on a piece of land next door to The Park orchard & Cobb nut plantation, Dad like most of the other men in the Hamlet during the war had an Allotment & after paying the rent tried hard to grow enough to keep us supplied all year round & so he could grow some flowers in the back garden. Potatoes were grown up there & then brought home in sacks on dad's bike (one on the handlebars &

two tied together over the crossbar), a Clamp was then made on the corner of the garden (not where the bucket had been emptied) a small area was trampled down wheat straw was put down the potatoes put in a pile then were covered with straw & then some soil to stop it blowing away (wheat straw was used because unlike Barley or Oat straw it doesn't absorb water), the same thing was also used for Carrots if you had a good crop. But after a few years got fed up with the local rabbits getting more of the produce than they were. We had great times in the shrubbery by the carriage drive to the Park, I remember one time particularly, as we were in the bushes we head some people talking as they were walking towards Eathorpe from the Park we thought as they had rather posh voices. So we made sure we couldn't be seen & started making owl noises by cupping our hands & blowing between the thumbs (you can also make more sounds by holding a blade of grass between your thumbs but have to be careful not to cut your lip). I don't know whether those folk really thought we were owls or just went along with it but one lady said "you don't normally hear owls this time of day, do you" we nearly gave ourselves away by laughing. Another game we played for a while was "Cherry Knocking" (knocking on peoples doors & hiding, particularly the door of the man who later stopped our bonfires, but we stopped that after a rather stern telling of from the local bobby (at least no clip round the ear, perhaps because there were a few of us). I could make bird sounds with my hands but I never ever learnt to whistle with my fingers, I tried & tried but it was one of my disappointments in life but not the end of the world. Later the shrubbery of The Hall would become our bike track. Like all kids we had our fall outs & fights, one day you were best friends, the next you could be fighting but it always seemed to "come out in the wash".

Sunday & goats

Sunday at one time was Sunday School Day, in the room by the shop, it was run by Mrs Fox (who was blind but no matter what you did, she somehow knew who the culprit was) I must admit I didn't enjoy it & was removed for pinning Shirley's plaits to her chair, it wasn't called Bullying then. I remember Choggy used to have to walk to Wappenbury every Sunday as he was payed a few pence, (that was very handy) to pump the Church organ for services & occasional Weddings (for which he got extra), some-times I went with him, which didn't always go down too well with the organist or the Vicar, as instead of watching the weight on the string, that had to be kept at the top by pumping the lever, two young lads behind the organ was always going to be a problem, as we would be mucking about & the weight would be at the bottom & the organist, had no air for the organ so she would be banging on the side of the organ, as she couldn't play the Hymn, then Choggy would pump like hell (Oops perhaps not the right expression for in a Church) for a bit! The weight would go up & the organ would burst into sound! Alas the Vicar decided, it was definitely not a good idea, for two of us to be there, so I was banned again. Perhaps I was a bit of rebel, no I was just a kid playing.

I occasionally used to walk with Bob Fox to Wappenbury where he used to milk goats for Miss Palmer-Hall, who had a field behind the Garage. I think the deal was, for doing the milking she let him have some, as he needed goat's milk for a skin condition, we didn't know about allergies then. The best bit was not trying to milk goats, though that stood me in good stead later on, but eating the flaked maize meant for the goats, that somehow was also a great snack for hungry young boys & was much the same as Kelloggs Corn Flakes!

Our Street

There wasn't any traffic to worry about on our street because the Fosse Way, (where after 1943 we used to see American Convoys go along on their way to or from the camp at Ryton on Dunsmore & we used to shout "got any gum chum?" & quite often getting some), looped around our street around by the pub. The only things you were liable to see were, the odd tractor either the orange Fordson or the smart new red International Farmall (driven by Chris, David's dad), a horse and cart, Mr Timms's coal lorry, Mrs Twist (from the Hall) in her white big Triumph Dolomite sports car that had two seats & a "dicky seat", you always kept a real eye on her because she had regular bumps (that kept Bert Williams busy repairing) & you never knew where she would go, or Mr Woodhouses's motorbike & side car (a Rudge I think). If he was on nights he was always about collecting wood for his fire (he was known as Mr Woodlouse) he & his wife spent hours scouring hedge rows for any dry wood & it was said they never bought coal. He was also our landlord's agent, so every week the rent had to be paid to him. I always enjoyed doing that because Mrs Woodhouse who always used the old Warwickshire way of saying yes as "OH Ahhh" & if she really meant it she would say "Oh Oh Oh Ahhh" made sweets & she always gave me two. The only regular vehicles were, the 7-45 Bus to Leamington Spa & the 5-45 return (if they turned up), the Post van. Luckily the postman knew everyone, as the houses were not numbered & only three had names, Farmer Hall from Princethorpe arrived about three o'clock in an old black car with milk churns in the back instead of seats.

Everyone went outside and he measured the milk into their jugs with a ladle, the milk jug would be put in a bucket with water in it, hoping it wouldn't be sour by the next afternoon, as no-one in our street had a fridge. I think he was paid weekly but I'm sure he knew who owed what & how many coupons to collect. If you worked on the farm you got your milk as part of your wages, so every day you would see the farm workers going home with their cans of milk. Another regular was the weekly visit of the International Stores van from Leamington Spa, bringing the grocery orders. We had a village shop but that was used for fags, papers and smaller bits that you didn't need coupons for, usually what mum had forgotten to put on the "International" list! When Mum went to the shop (Dad never did) she always used to say as a joke "I'm off to get a Pattet of Tea & a Stware of Bwoo" mimicking an old friend of hers who had a speech impediment. As it was war time you basically had what they had in stock. The one thing they always seemed to have in stock was Apricot jam I got so I hated the stuff, (which meant I didn't have bread & jam unless just occasionally we had Pineapple jam which dad reckoned was swede with pineapple flavour but I liked that) I always preferred bread & pork dripping with loads of brown gravy & salt if mum could get some & of course a tin of Spam. Dad always said the Cheese was just "Bunghole & even the mice didn't like it & that's why we never caught too many in the mouse trap" Mum like others was always juggling the ration coupons & always changed our butter ration with someone for margarine so we had more, though it was always a joke that she used to put it on & scrape it off again & when she made jam tarts it was hunt the jam. Mum did make jam but it usually went mouldy. The nearest Butcher's Shop was at Matron, so Mum & everyone else from surrounding villages had to walk there & hope he had got some meat if only Scrag End or a bit of Belly Pork I can't remember having Beef & never saw a piece of Steak till I was well grown up. The Baker used to come from Long Itching ton in a little Ford Van once a week, (we never had the lovely Black Crusts like Chioggia's Mum, I now wonder if she had those loaves because they were burnt & cheaper but it was amazing how we happened to be at Choggie's when the baker arrived) The other regular was every other week the big red lorry would arrive, with soaps particularly Carbolic, washing flakes & powder, boxes of Thermogene to put on your chest to keep warm, sometimes you would have a vest made of this stuff if you had a bad chest. There was also dish cloths, mops, brushes, nails & screws, hob nails for the soles & metal tips for toes & heels on boots, candles, wicks, lamp-glasses, polish, black lead for the range & if they could be found batteries for bike lights etc. & at the back was a tank of Paraffin with the big measuring cans, I can still smell that lorry now & it was like a mobile Aladdin's Cave, in fact I bet even the driver didn't know about some of the things in it. Another sight in Eathorpe was the Chimney Sweep, Mrs Quinney. She lived at Princethorpe & travelled round on a bike, with a trailer behind full of brushes sheets & bags of soot (that's if the customer didn't want it for the garden). What a character, a big lady with a huge voice & smile (or was it just her teeth showing on her sooty face?) & could she swear, most of us learnt a lot from her! We all loved Mrs Quincey, she would turn out for weddings (for a small fee) because in those days it was considered lucky. I can remember her being at my sister Nina's wedding. Is that why there are so many divorces now? Chimney Sweeps are few & far between!

Home grown food

We nearly always kept chickens down the garden & sometimes a pig!, always called "Peggy". I remember Dad winning one in a bowling contest. The pig & chickens lived on scraps, stuff off the garden or allotment & corn Mum got Gleaning (Gleaning was done just after harvest, with permission you would pick up heads of corn off the ground before the farmer turned stock into the field.) When the hens stopped laying we had chicken for Sunday dinner & the cockerel usually met his fate at Christmas. When the time came for the pig to be slaughtered, Dad's friend would come from Marton on his motor-bike & sidecar, Dad would get two trusses of straw & put them on a clear patch of garden. We kids must have been a blood thirsty lot, as we stood & watched as the pig was led out of the sty squealing like mad. Then being held by Dad the pig's throat would be cut. The poor thing would squeal for ages before falling down. Mum always made sure she was missing at this time. Then us kids took it in turns to pump the legs to get the blood out, once it was done the straw was lit to burn off the bristles. I know it now seems barbaric but that was the way it was done & I know us kids didn't grow up any the worse for being there.

When you had a pig killed you lost your meat ration but you gained a lot of friends, including the local kids because if the butcher was careful & removed the bladder without damage, after drying, it became a good

Football. The carcase was hung on the steel rod that I used for" Tarzan swings" as I got older. The rod held the kitchen to the rest of the house. A bowl placed under the carcase to catch the rest of the blood. It was quite weird walking by it to get to the sink in the kitchen & a bath at night was definitely out. As we had neither fridge nor freezer any meat that was not going to be salted had to be eaten, so friends who liked Chitlins were happy to clean them (intestines they looked horrible) & other bits of offal & meat went into other people's pantries. Mum used to make lovely brawn from the pig's head. Home cured & cut bacon is totally different to what you buy in a shop, OK it is usually a bit fatty & about a quarter of an inch thick (not unlike the slices of belly Pork you buy from the butchers) but the taste is yum, Our tin bath was filled with water & salt to make brine & the meat left to soak in it for ages (no baths for a while) Then the hams etc. were treated with Salt Peter before being hung on hooks on the kitchen wall. I bet unless that wall has been replaced you can still see the shape of those hams now!

Our Village

Eathorpe in those days had (coming from Wappenbury) on the left The Water mill, a big house (not sure who lived there but I think it was some-one who owned a factory near Dunchurch), Mr Tooley's house, Three cottages I have forgotten who lived there & the Telephone Box (yes I know it was not a house but for us kids it was the main meeting place, where occasionally a pane of glass would get broken & we would make sure we were not around, when the "local policeman" who lived four miles away at Weston under Wetherley, came on his "round" either on his pushbike or later a Vellocette? LE water cooled & very quiet motor bike that was a bit quicker than his push-bike. A police-man then had to be over six feet tall plus his helmet, so he was always an imposing figure & because of this he looked a bit scary. You respected or was scared of him & he knew most of us. When the Telephone Box was lit after the war, it was the only street light we had. There was then The Blacksmiths shop, The Shop & Sunday School (which was a Corrugated Iron building). There were then two houses one of which was the Post Office (Mrs Hoggins), a House behind (Mr & Mrs Fox) their house had a huge garden that stretched from the street right down to the river bank, two houses (Mrs Ball) & a tied house that went with Mr Penteloes farm. Our house, Mr & Mrs Williams, Mr & Mrs Woodhouse then their daughter lived in the next, then two thatched houses the end one Mr & Mrs Timms the Coal Merchant. On the other side of the road, two thatched cottages with a water pump the other side of the Fosse Way (Pauline lived in the in the first), four houses in a row (Oonagh who lived opposite me & when we were very small used to call to each other from bedroom windows! I think her Dad was the Gardener at the Park) (Shirley) (David) & a tied house for Flannel Reeve's farm, that house changed hands regularly. A big house that looked a bit like a chapel, it was then used as a Land Army Hostel. Where some of the older lads (Scrogger, Alf, Fred, Ray & Brian & some of the married men, got quite "friendly" with the girls. Those girls did sterling work on farms all over the UK. There was Mr Reeve's (known as Flannel) huge farm house & out buildings one of which Julie & Eric moved to, around the Fosse Way loop there was a thatched cottage Percy & Gwen (there were ten in their family), & the pub called The Plough. This is where my dad went every night, Saturday & Sunday lunchtimes, as did a few others from the village & two from Princethorpe. He always had a fresh flower in his buttonhole kept fresh by water in a small container that he made at work that was pinned behind his collar always having three Pints of Ansell's Mild, when that was not available Northampton Brewery Company used to deliver dad said it was rubbish. The company should have been called NBG not NBC, but he still drank it! Thinking back that's perhaps why we never had much, mother used to say "you are putting a fur coat on Mrs Rance's back but I haven't got a shilling for the meter". (She always had a foreign coin to put in at those times & had it back in the "divi"). Some times in the winter we kids would go to the pub with our dads & we were allowed in the kitchen, where we played I Spy while drinking our one bottle of Vimto or Lemonade or sometimes Dandelion & Burdock. In the summer we played on the lawn of the pub but were not allowed to play with a ball (too many windows). Next was the Park Lodge (where Mr & Mrs Sparkes lived, who had a daughter in the Land Army & a son in Army. They also had a daughter who was called "slow" but she was lovely & I'm sure there was a proper name for it) that stood at the entrance, to the long carriage drive for The Park that stood in a beautiful parkland & like the Hall had two entrances, one for the Family & Guests, the other at the rear for Tradesmen. This was the road or drive that we used to get to Marton. The first part went with the Park & was closed for one day a year with a big white gate by the Lodge, the second part was really a farm road & then an access to Robson's farm from Marton. Toward Princethorpe were two houses, one where the butler come handy-man for the Park lived with his brother, one down the fields (later Eric & Julie). Toward Hunningham the Hall lodge where on a summers evening Ray would sit outside playing his Accordion, it used to sound lovely all over the hamlet because there was little or no traffic noise. Next The Stables flats & The Hall. Until 1959 when I moved away there had only been three new buildings, one in the old coal yard that was built for George (Joe's brother), the replacement building for Choggies thatched cottage a building that caused a lot of discussion of what it was to be when built & a Wooden Village Hall built on part of the field donated by Mrs Twist where Brian kept his cows, my twenty first Birthday Party being the first event in it.

Wash day

Wash day was always on Monday! & you never ever washed on a Sunday even if it was the only dry day of the week, it was almost a Cardinal Sin to hang washing out on Sunday. Our kitchen comprised of the Black Range, & the Copper at the end, a sink under the window, then a gap that was filled some years later with a Burko Electric Boiler, an Electric Cooker that was mostly used when the Range wasn't lit & a table opposite the Cooker with Dining Chairs under & just enough room for the tin Bath to fit in-between. The water would be collected, the copper would be lit, kept well stoked & the water boiled. The galvanized Bath was brought out of the toilet into the kitchen & hot water put in from the copper, soap flakes (when you could get them) or powder was added & after a good stir the clothes were put in & worked round with a "Bosher" & if there were any stains, the offending article was put in a bowl of soapy water & then rubbed with Carbolic or Fairy Soap on the wash board (the same type of board that became a musical instrument in the days of Skiffle), there was also the Blue Bag that was as small muslin bag with a square of Blue in it & was dipped in the water for the whites, (it was also used to rub on wasp & bee stings & it did help). Mum had a little Mangle that could be clamped on the kitchen table with a bowl on the floor to mangle the clothes but it was a bit small so, she used to go next door where Mr & Mrs Williams lived after lodging with us & use their old big Mangle with wooden rollers that stood in their yard. (In fact a lot of the people in our row of houses used that mangle I think it went with the house!) Snook also one day thought it would be a good idea to put his elder brother Robert's fingers through the mangle, his backside was warmed up for that, his backside was warmed up regularly but it never seemed to bother him (he was known as the little bugger, Mum called him a "Buggeroota", I'm sure they would call it something else now perhaps something quite scientific). Occasionally Mum would starch collars which meant the Robin Starch powder was mixed with water (no spray stuff then) collars dipped in & ironed if you used the iron too hot the starch went brown. The clothes would then be hung on the line down the garden. Mum always had an Electric Iron & plugged it into a double adaptor on the front room light, she had some old flat irons that you put in front of the fire to heat up but never used them. Her ironing was a bit like her needle work but we got by. One of the jobs on Tuesday I helped with when I was small, if the washing were dry, was helping fold sheets & I got quite good at that! There was also an old Clothes Horse that was used in front of the kitchen range for drying things that were needed quick but sometimes got scorched & when Margaret lived at home, it was nearly always something belonging to her!

Fight Fight

When Nina got married she moved to Doncaster as her husband (Jack) worked on the Railways. Which meant there was comparative peace at home because when Nina & Margaret were both at home they fought like cat & dog, usually because Nina had "borrowed" something belonging to Margaret if she was going to a dance at a pub at Ryton where the Yanks from the camp used to go. They were amazing, even if they had identical jobs Margaret always had money but Nina was usually skint by the end of the week! I sometimes used to think that perhaps before she was married Nina was a bit jealous of Margaret because Joe used to come & see Margaret most nights but Nina's Jack was in Doncaster. In those days lots of farmers used to grow Cabbage for their cows (they were larger than those grown in the garden), occasionally Joe's mum would cook one for her family (well they were there). They were at least one step up from Brussels & if Joe let go with a "quiet one" Oh my G-d what a stink you could not only smell it you could nearly see a green cloud! Nina was the one who mixed the Peroxide & bleached her hair & had a scare when it started falling out. Margaret was now working at Manders at Leamington, which was handy if dad wanted to do a bit of decorating as it was a wallpaper & paint store. I did say comparative peace but alas Margaret & Dad used to regularly fall out, when he either wanted to cadge some cash or borrow her bike! Eventually she moved in with Joe, after another bust up with Dad (after he left the Lockheed he worked as a gardener for Mrs Twist at the Hall which meant he was paid monthly, he was regularly short of money when he was paid weekly, so being paid monthly was a total nightmare). Which left me all alone with Mum & Dad & it was a bit difficult because Mum & Dad didn't know where she had gone but she always kept in touch with me. Yes my two sisters always looked out for their little brother. In fact the only photo of me growing up was taken in a little Motor Boat when I went for a week's holiday at Skegness with Nina & Jack in a caravan at Butlins when I was 14 years old I think. Which was quite an adventure because first I had to go to Rugby then catch a train to Skegness which meant spending a night on Rugby railway station because of connections & then the same on the way back.

Our River Leam

The River Leam always was & I'm sure still is a major part of the community. To control the water for The Mill, a Leat was formed under the road, & a Flood-gate controlled the flow as the river naturally went round a bend. Alas in the winter the Flood-gate sometimes became overwhelmed & parts of the Village were flooded. As the Mill was no longer used, I can never remember there being a wheel. The Flood-gate was removed & a small water-fall built between the walls, & a larger one next to it. Which meant the water didn't come up the road into the village when there was a flood. The pool directly below the old Flood-gate then became the Eathorpe Pool, the bank & an Island were bequeathed to the Community for recreational use. The Island could only be reached by crossing the two water-falls, paddling through the shallow end of the Pool, or jumping over the narrow stream that formed one side of the island, also fed by a small Water-fall about two hundred yards from the Pool. Just before the Island the river went round a big bend which made a big pool known as Grove Pool. There were no rushes there as the water was so deep. It was said that an underwater stream crossed there. Many of us as we grew older & or more stupid, tried to get to the bottom holding bricks in our hands but to no avail. The Island was covered in Willow trees that had currant bushes growing on the top of the trunks & many a time, young stomachs were upset by either eating too many or too soon. There was also long grass & a few brambles. Every year there would be a swan's nest & we knew to keep well clear when the Cob or Pen were sitting or when there were

Cygnets because they could be quite violent. Or, on a sunny day, if you saw two adults in the long grass who definitely wanted to be left alone. You most certainly knew that was the time to keep well away!

The Pool was where we all learnt to swim (well nearly all). It was about six feet deep near the Flood-gate wall then gradually shallower till the paddling bit near the road bridge, this is also where the stream joined. The bank between the road & the Pool on a sunny Sunday afternoon would be packed with families not only from Eathorpe but people would arrive by car to enjoy our Lido. Using the Flood-gate deck we would stand around, sometimes shivering, daring each other to jump or dive off the side walls about eight feet high. How wonderful it was to swim under water & see fish scurrying away, or swimming between the girls legs! As the water came over the moss covered water-fall it was filtered but we never thought about that. When it became too cold for swimming or generally mucking about, it was time for fishing. If you couldn't "borrow" your dads rod, a cane or a piece of hazel, a bit of line, a stripped crow's feather held on the line with two bits of bike valve rubber & a bent pin was our kit, using Cadis fly for bait, OK so we never caught anything big but we had good times trying. The only photo I have of me as a young child, is one taken at the pool with me in a Bathing Costume! We didn't have Budgie Smuggling trunks then.

The Leam was well known for fishing & the fishing rights from different farmer's land were owned by Fishing Clubs (that didn't bother us kids). Dad became the Water Bailiff for the stretch between Eathorpe & Princethorpe bridge for a Coventry Club (expect he got free fishing) so he would walk the river bank checking licenses, on Sunday morning during the fishing season, before he went to the pub. He would spend hours crushing stale bread crusts that he had baked in the oven with Mum's rolling pin. He used the crumbs as "Ground

Bait" to draw the Roach & Chubb he then made his Bate out of Bread, Flour & a bit of Custard Powder (if Mum had got any) he would mix it in a bowl with a little water so it was just thick enough to stay on the hook. He never used Worms or Caddis Larva, because he didn't fish for Perch or Pike. He never used a Reel (though he had one) but just fixed his line to his rod. Then if the weather was good would go back in the afternoon after having his dinner (still in his sports coat, flannels & shirt & tie) & have a sleep in the sun on the bank. There was such an array of fish in our river from Sticklebacks, Minnows, Millers Thumbs (Bully Heads), Gudgeon (the fish I was named after, I always thought it was because I as a good swimmer, but perhaps it was because they are not very big, not good looking & are easily caught. perhaps I'll stick with the first bit), Dace, Roach, Bream & the two predators Perch & Pike (a Pike's mouth is just full of very sharp teeth & if you caught one you had to be very careful or it would have your fingers).

Hunningham C of E School

Anyway I digress! I didn't start school till I was six (No I don't know why "perhaps I was away driving my lorry") I remember my first day, going on my three wheel trike (second hand) with mum by my side, going the long way round on the gated road to Hunningham, because the trike couldn't take the short cut across the fields with my square box on my chest & a strap round my neck with my Gas Mask in. It was about three miles from home. The gated road was & still is a single track road that turned off the Fosse way just past Mr Clarke's farm house & after six gates came out in Hunningham. We soon learnt that the Gated Road was the place where people came in cars on Thursday afternoon (early closing in Leamington) to get shall we say "amorous" even in wartime when petrol was rationed, obviously enough could be found. It was there that Mr Penelope, who farmed that land used to move them on when they parked on the field. We regularly used to see him in his top coat & trilby hat walking his fields checking the stock, you always knew when he was around even if he was the other side of a hedge, because there would be a cloud of smoke from the pipe he always had in his mouth.

The short cut was a footpath with a Kiss-gate at the road the across the corner of the marsh field, then a stile at the Hazel nut hedge. Across a meadow (when that was shut for hay we went round the edge & along the Crab-apple & Pig Pear hedge. Then over a Style by the third gate & onto the Gated Road.

I first met Mrs Somerton who taught the infants, then Mrs Gilpin who taught the seven to ten, then the Head-master Mr Helm who taught everyone else till they left school (unless you passed the eleven plus). I now realise indomitable Mrs Somerton, was just as you would imagine a School Ma'am, she rode an Auto Cycle (a very early & cumbersome moped) from Radford Semele every day come rain or shine. Anyway I think I enjoyed my first day at school even though I got shouted at for wiping my nose on my sleeve (a bad habit which I soon stopped after she said she would call me "silver sleeve"), it seemed funny eating my dinner with the other children as I had never really done that before. I must admit I was pleased to see mum waiting for me at four o'clock to go home, I think back now that meant she walked twelve miles that day! The next day I walked to school with the others being looked after by Shirley she was nearly eight! Walking along the road then through the fields & then on the gated road, through one very mucky farm yard & then through Hunningham to the school. Quite often arriving in very wet & muddy shoes & feet as most of us didn't own wellies. I like others sometimes had cardboard in my shoes because there was a hole that Dad couldn't get a bit of leather to nail on, using his old "snobbing iron," as there were no coupons for new ones even if there was money. A trip we would do for years, till finally we were allowed to use the Leamington bus. For me only about one year. Mrs Somerton taught us how to count, she taught us the Alphabet by reciting it forwards & backwards & yes it worked (I can still recite it backwards today) we learnt & recited times tables, we played with Plasticise, made bags out of mesh & raffia & also to knit. But the best bit was when she read us the letters that her son sent her, he was a Submariner & even though some bits were cut out we sat enthralled hanging on to every word & even though we didn't understand what conditions must have been like, we wanted to be submariners. As far as I know he was one of the lucky one to survive. We had milk in the morning in little bottles with a cardboard top, that if you didn't press in in correctly, you got covered in milk. Those cardboard tops would be used to make pom-poms using oddments of wool.

Hunningham School had two rooms, Mrs Somerton had the small room, and then Mrs Gilpin had part of the larger room, with Mr Helm having the rest. There was a playground next to the Church yard, & a field we were allowed to play in provided there were no cattle around, with an old Fullers Earth pit, a bit away from the school, where the older pupils got up to things we didn't know about, then! The School was nearly self-sufficient as there was a garden where pupils had plots & grew most of what the school needed (there was a prize at the end of the year for the best plot). There were rabbits, chickens & a tame jackdaw, (that had been taught to speak, after its tongue was split) in runs in the playground. The school dinners were cooked in Mr Helm's kitchen by Granny Russell and I loved them, except the cabbage. You didn't leave the table till your plate was empty & it was worth eating the cabbage, so you could have some of her jam roly-poly or treacle pud with custard, I can still taste it now! Not long after starting school I started getting sore throats regularly & the doctor said I needed my tonsils removing, so mother took me into Warneford Hospital at Leamington Spa by bus. For the first time in my life I wore pyjamas. Alas I was sick overnight, so I was sent home for a week. Getting from Eathorpe to Leamington when you didn't have a car, was difficult to say the least! Mother took me in a week later & the offending items were removed, the best bit was the jelly & ice cream afterwards. You were kept in Hospital for five days then, all this was all paid for by "the hospital fund "that was paid into monthly. Mum visited every day I was in hospital, she was a trooper. There being a bus 7 45 & a return at from Leamington at 4 45, which meant she was in Leamington all day just for an hour with me. That put the end to days off school through a bad throat! Shirley had appendicitis & had to have an operation to remove her Appendix, & when she came home we were all so keen to see her scar, especially us lads as she always pulled her knickers right down to show us. David had Scarlett Fever, that it was said was caught from the drain at the Land Army hostel. He was my best friend & I missed him so much while he was in hospital & that really was all the major ills we had then. Brenda fell off a bike in the Shrubbery & the brake lever went into her Groin & she had to have stitches but was soon back on it. Of course just like all kids I had Mumps, Measles (German & ordinary) Coughs, Colds, in fact if there was anything going around I usually got it. Most things meant staying indoors for a while & having your chest rubbed with Vick where appropriate & cuts treated with Germolene.

We fell from trees, fell off bikes (regularly), we all had scrapes & bruises but we must have had strong bones as no-one broke anything (they breed 'em tough in Warwickshire)

The two school rooms were heated with a round Anthracite cast iron boiler in each room, stoked by monitors. If there was snow, a snowball put on top of the boiler created such a stink, it was almost worth getting the cane for. The cane was used for all types of misdemeanours, usually going in the Church yard without permission, Hunningham Church is a Saxon Church with a wooden tower & the whole school went for a service on Ascension Day & on Remembrance Day. Making paper aeroplanes was all the rage the &If you had made one that flew well, & it flew into the church yard, of course you wanted it back & it was worth risking the cane to retrieve it. We younger pupils were not caned that hard but you always wanted to go to the toilet so you could have a cry, because you wanted to look brave, even though it hurt. The toilets being two small buildings one for boys one for girls. Inside there was a board with a hole & a long drop, there was a roll of Izal paper and a sink with a jug of water that had to be topped up at playtime.

Occasionally we would be told to take our Gas Masks next day to school so we could practise making sure we knew how to use them properly & twice a week we had PT in the playground if it wasn't raining too hard & every night we had a prayer & sang the National Anthem before we went home. One morning on the way to school, in the second field of the gated road, we came across thousands of strips of silver paper that were like bigger versions of the coloured strips we made Christmas chains out of. We thought we had discovered something really exciting, we felt like real spies. So we gathered a few bits up & took them to school. They turned out to have been an experiment that had been dropped from a plane to interfere, with the new thing called Radar. Those bits were very quickly picked up by the local Home Guard. We later found a huge Balloon with a little box attached & imagined it to be something real secret at least & was quite disappointed to find it was just a Weather Balloon the local bobby collected that.

One time there was a bus going from Eathorpe to a Circus near Rugby I think it was Dunchurch & I was so excited Mum had got us tickets. Alas at school the day before, my belly started to itch, so I went to the toilet to have a look (& a scratch) & my belly was covered in big spots. When I got home because I was scratching Mum had a look & I had Chicken Pox! So that meant no Circus for me even though I pleaded, cried & stamped my feet (I got a whack for that). No school for three weeks. The nearest doctor lived at Stretton on Dunsmore but once a week held a surgery in a house at Marton, later changed to a room at Princethorpe once a week. Being ill meant once a week walking to the surgery or waiting till the Doctor could come out to you, (that Doctor earned his money which until 1948 you had to pay monthly.) Being isolated meant going to the telephone kiosk ringing the Doctor & hoping.

Some Big Milestones

Reaching eight years old was a milestone in my life, as Dad decided I should go to Murray Road School in Rugby because he went there & so did Bob, I definitely did not want to go but had no choice. When I left Hunningham School I was presented with a Penknife. When you left to go to work the girls were given a Handbag & the boys a Wallet by Mr Helm. To get to Murray Road School, meant leaving home well before seven, riding my very second hand bike down the Park Carriage drive to Marton, leaving my bike at a house in the village, then walking about a mile along the main Coventry to Banbury road to the railway station, one of the exciting things about that walk was, occasionally you would see & hear a steam lorry, laden with cement. The sound of the drive chains humming was incredible & then returning the process at night getting home about seven. I hated Murray Road School after being at Hunningham, where I knew every-one. Going to such a big town school was horrible. The train arrived early enough so that us kids who walked through the cattle market to school, regularly stood & watched calves & sheep being slaughtered (blood thirsty lot). Then buying a warm bread roll from the bakers in Railway Terrace, next door to where Bob worked (Jimmy Malin's) before joining the army. Occasionally I would stay at Grans on a Friday Night (having to sleep in her bed, didn't like that), so I could go to the Grenada to the Saturday Morning Rush (I was a Grenada Grenadier.) A time to catch up on the adventures of Roy Rodgers & Trigger, Hopalong Cassidy, Gene Autry, The Bowery Boys, who wore their baseball caps side-ways or back to front to look daft (they say there is nothing new in fashion), Laurel & Hardy & of course Tarzan & Jane with their animals.

After about six months that school nearly destroyed me & Dad saw sense because he was paying the train fare & I returned to Hunningham & I was not only delighted to be back with my friends, but I was also allowed to keep my Penknife.

When any of us kids had been to the pictures we used to recreate the story in the shrubbery, with whoever saw the film as the star of course. Cor, the amount of Indians that got chased through that shrubbery by the Cowboys was incredible, considering just how few of us kids there were. Occasionally we would go to Marton Village Hall if they had a U certificate film. It was always a great time with the film sometimes breaking or the projector breaking down & you had to wait halfway through the film for the reel to be changed but it was very cheap! & it gave us the chance to learn something we thought might be useful from the antics of some the adults on the sofas at the back!

Holidays

Reaching Eight also meant I could go potato picking up at Kenning's farm & get a bit of pocket money (Joe's mum, she used to scare me, you daren't miss any spuds). I was also old enough to go on a camping holiday. Every year Mr Helm took boys on holiday (it was said he tried to take girls also once but they got very homesick) those of us whose parents could or would afford Fifteen Shillings could go for a week's camping in Wales. Mr Helm had a big Armstrong Sidley car with a column gear change, which he worked with his false arm (he lost his arm during WW1). Eight or ten of us kids fitted in the car (somehow) & a trailer carried the camping kit (which belonged to Mr Helm). This time we had to go via Newcastle under Lyme as Mr Helm had some business to do. When we arrived at the farm, where we were due to camp over-night at it was raining cats and dogs. So the farmer let us sleep in the barn, Mr Helm slept in the farm-house. There was hay to fill our Paillasses, obviously the older boys getting the best of course, us younger ones had a few thistles in ours, so we bunked down for the night. It was then a couple of the older lads started throwing boots around & I got one on the side of my head, I think the worst bit was not the pain but making sure no-one saw me cry (even though I wanted to). But next morning all was forgotten except for a little lump on the side of my head, when we were invited into the farm kitchen for breakfast. Lovely eggs & thick bread with Butter on. After emptying the hay from our Paillasses, I am sure the cattle still enjoyed it after our use. When we finally arrived at Llandudno we pitched the two large tents & Mr Helms small tent. We again filled our Paillasses, then dug a hole for the Latrine Tent & cut out a square of turf for the fire. The jobs were dished out, collecting water, collecting milk & bread, cooking & washing up etc. The farm we camped at was at Penryhn, so to get to Llandudno you caught a tram. It was from that tram (I loved those trams even though the fare ate into my spending money), after passing the Little Orme I first saw the sea, Wow. The sight of those waves & the shingly beach was for a midlands country kid almost unbelievable. After getting off the tram it was a mad rush to the beach off with the shoes & a paddle in the water (remember in those days boys wore short trousers & girls didn't wear trousers. In fact, I never had long trousers till I went to Grammar School). After paddling it was off to the shops & little arcades to spend our days ration of spending money, making sure we had left enough for the tram back to camp. As food was still rationed then, we had to bring coupons with us on holiday, but Mr Helm always saved up some of his meat ration, so we could have an enormous tin of Corned-beef & we had all sorts of meals using it. We spent time climbing The Little Orme but not The Great Orme because you had to pay to go on there. Taking our bathing costumes (yes most of us didn't have trunks) we braved the sea even though it always seemed colder than our River Leam, diving into waves & coming up spluttering, oh that taste of salt water. Yes we certainly had a great time. One of the extra pleasures we had was a free trip to the Pictures usually seeing a Cowboy film. I remember one night we were queuing outside the Cinema & a lady asked Fred where he came from & he was amazed she hadn't heard of Hunningham Hill!(well it was the centre of his world) We have laughed with Fred about that many times over the years.

Because of modern Laws Mr Helm would not now have been able to take us kids on holiday, being an elderly single man, with only one arm & all of us in that big old car, but I went on great holidays with that wonderful

Man many times & I can definitely say "he was the perfect Gentleman" even if we had to do as we were told. Like most of us, if it wasn't for Mr Helm we would never had holidays (I never went on holiday with my parents) Shirley always went on holiday with her parents & when she came home she used to show us tram tickets from all over the place including Blackpool where she described all the shows she had seen & the Circus, Oh yes we were jealous.

On my third holiday to Llandudno I saw & was a passenger on my first ship, (being a country kid I had never seen a ship other than in a book or a film) she was the St Tudor a rusty old tub based at Liverpool, but to me she was my Queen Mary. We went from Llandudno to the Menia Bridge & round Puffin Island (Never knowing that 70 years later I would be standing on Ilfracombe Pier as the Town Crier, in the same colour coat that I saw the bombing of Coventry in, yes a Red one with a Black Collar! greeting ships the Balmoral & PS Waverley that do that very same trip today) the trip on the Steamer & the Pictures all came out of the 15 shillings along with the food, fuel & field! What a man Mr Helm was? They don't make people like him anymore, he was not just a school teacher, he was someone we loved & all turned to at times & incredibly he always seemed to have the right answer.

The Moon Lady

One year we went to Aberdovey for a change & camped at a farm above The Outward Bound School. It happened to be a farm that kept quite a few pigs & they were fed on boiled swill (kitchen waste collected from round the area & stored in steel drums) & the smell was always there. After doing our usual chores (there was one chore less as Mr Helm then had a caravan, as he was getting too old to get up from the ground). We excitedly walked down to the harbour. To do so we had to walk through the School orchard, after being warned not to, you still had to try an apple even though you knew they were nowhere near ripe. It was in that orchard us lads saw this apparition, a young lady, who perhaps had an effect on us for the rest of our lives. We christened her "The Moon Lady" she was about nineteen or twenty, with everything appearing to us to be in the right places, wearing a white dress with a moon pattern on. We were of the age when our hormones were getting active. We only saw her twice or three times but there was a lot of fervent shuffling under our blankets, after just thinking of her. Years after those of us that are left, when reminiscing about our holidays, we have had many a laugh about our Goddess "the Moon Lady". Aberdovey was the first place we had ever seen Glow worms. We were fascinated, that such a small bug could make a light. So it seemed a great idea to collect a few put them in a jam-jar, then we would have a light in the tent. Alas it didn't work, just like lots of school boy ideas. Mr Helm then explained that they flashed their lights to attract a mate & they obviously did not do that in a jam-jar! Oh well it seemed like a good idea &

would have been good if it worked. It was also here that we found out Choggie sleep walked. On about the second night we were fast asleep when something was climbing over us & then walked out of the tent (we always left a bit of the flap open, in case someone needed to wee) he wandered round a bit then returned. Next morning we made sure he moved his bed next to the tent flap, he didn't do it every night but it was not unusual & really weird. As there was no cinema at Aberdovey we were treated to a visit to a travelling Circus, the first & only time I have seen a 3 legged Goose & 2 headed Chicken. We spent hours trying to catch Flatties off the pier & generally having a great time in the water. There were no waves like at Llandudno & the water wasn't any warmer but if you thought of "the Moon Lady" you didn't notice.

As the years ran on & we got older & bigger & Mr Helm retired, he stopped taking new kids, but nearly all of the "old crew" still went. By now he was using a caravan as he couldn't sleep on the ground. The two tents & gear were loaded in the caravan hooked up to the Armstrong Sidley then off we went, but as there was not so much room in the car, a few of us used to ride in the caravan. Mr Helm telling us "Now don't you dare look out of the windows when going through a town or village, because you are not supposed to be in there"? This made the holiday even more exciting for a bunch of boys. Mr Helm always smoked hand rolled tipped cigarettes, he used "white horse tobacco" that was in a white box with papers, tips & rolling machine, normally he could roll his fags with one hand but on holiday there was always a volunteer to roll them. He knew not every fag rolled went into the box & there was a few fervent puffs each from the illicit fag but was quite happy to let us kids feel clever. Of course there were wet days when we would stay in the tent & listen to the rain on the canvas, making sure we didn't touch the roof in case it made it leak.

For years we used to borrow Mr Helm's tents & camp in Eathorpe for most of the summer holiday in a field near the small waterfall, girls (Oonagh, Julie Shirley Jack & Jill) in one & us boys (Choggy, David, Eric & Me) in the other. We didn't have paillasses so we slept on the ground sheet & had an old blanket for cover. Of course there were fall-outs but we always got over them. Sometimes my Dad would join us boys for a week or so after work, but he always had to go to the pub! Going home when we ran out of food or milk. We tried cooking the fish we caught in the river, Yuc a little Perch or Roach certainly had more bones than meat, & a Miller's thumb (or Bully Head) or Gudgeon was even worst. But a potato or onion put in a fire, then taken out when it was black usually tasted OK, well we thought it did even if a tad smoky.

Things you learn

Living "in the wilds" meant we learnt so much about nature. Sometimes from Choggies Mum who knew so much about wild life & plants, particularly wild birds & eggs. I don't know where she learnt it from but she really was incredible. We learnt the difference between Frog & Toad Spawn & how to keep Tadpoles. To watch them grow into frogs. Toad Spawn was difficult to collect as it was in strings attached to a weed. We learnt the difference from a Carrion Crow that nested alone, a Rook that nested in a Rookery at the top of tall trees (that meant a Rook's egg was a rarity) or a Jackdaw that nested in chimneys & holes in trees not just by their looks but also their calls. The difference between a Magpie's nest & a Squirrels dray (they both have roofs & you would get a painful surprise when reaching for an egg if a Squirrel was at home). The difference between a Moor-hen & a Coot by the bit of white. We learnt that a Chaffinch's call was "pink pink pink", a Yellowhammer's call sounded like "a little bit of bread & no cheese" We learnt what "Pied" meant as in Pied Wagtail or Pied Horse {Black & White}, We knew the difference between a Song Thrush that sang beautifully & a Mistle Thrush known as a Storm Cock because it always sang on the highest branch possible before a storm. The Blackbird that song beautifully but like the Jay was also the guardian of the woods & would cry an alarm if predators (even little boys) were around. We knew the Skylark from its song & also vertical flight & hover. The Lapwings cry of "Pee wit" gave it its common name, the lapwing like the Skylark never landed or took flight from their nest always running along the ground to hide it. The shrill song of the Robin & Jenny Wren how such a small bird can make that sound was incredible. Perhaps the most incredible sound of all was that of the Nightingale, to hear its song across the woods was breath taking & is world famous. There was also the Cuckoo who's call we all tried to copy & in the evening & early morning the Little Owl could be heard setting out his territory (we copied that very well by cupping our hands & blowing through our thumbs & many a time, got passers- by confused from our position in a bush we knew the difference between a Barn Owl, a Tawny Owl & a Little Owl). The bird that could get us all confused was the Starling as they could mimic most bird's songs, they are super intelligent. We learnt the difference between Swallows, Swifts & House-martens. I know it's not a cry but the sound of a Wood-pecker drumming on a hollow branch is something special. There were so many others that chirped, whistled or sang & there were not many we didn't know.   But no matter how clever we thought we were with birds, we could never understand how a little Betty Hedge-sparrow would take on a Cuckoo's egg & raise its chick even though it kicked the Betties chicks out of the nest. We also learned how to kill a Rabbit with a sharp tap behind the ears with the edge of your hand or just a pull of the neck both methods worked instantly, you also learnt that if you cut it's belly immediately the innards fell out but if you let it get cold you had to pull them out, we learnt how to cut the skin behind the joint on the back leg & thread the opposite paw through so it could be hung up & also how to skin a Rabbit, (there was occasionally a Rag & Bone man who came round collecting Rabbit skins) some people carried a paw for luck. We learnt to tell what animal had been around by the paw marks it left on the ground or snow for instance a Fox's paw marks are always in a straight line. We looked even closer after seeing a film about "the Indians" tracking or even Tarzan.

Back to school & more country kid's stuff

I remember once at school when there was a "mass caning of four boys" after it was found out that Mrs Gilpin was scared of mice, so a dead mouse was put on her desk & it didn't take long to find the culprits! (I was not one of them) Mr Helm always administered the cane. Boys or girls had it on the backside, & what was incredible we all "thought the world" of that man, (to me he was perhaps the "grandad" I needed), no matter how many times you had the cane. One day Charlie (who lived in the Farm with the muddy gate) was being given the cane & started yelling "stop, stop I'm peeing myself) he was & it took a while to get over his embarrassment. The girls at one time had a craze of cutting their initials in their book covers with razor blades & I think most finished up having the cane, more than once. It was the time when the pupils stayed at the School till they started work at fourteen. Some of the older lads, really, had the cane. One I remember for taking a Swan's egg. In those days we all collected birds eggs but we knew the country code only one from each nest & check it in water first, if it sank it was OK, if not you put it back, because the chick had started to form. The only exceptions were moorhens, as so long as you left one egg they would keep laying for ever! Usually collecting Moorhens eggs with a spoon tied to a hazel stick, & moorhen's eggs are delicious even though smaller than hen's. During the spring nearly all the eggs mum used for cooking were moorhens. We learnt how to blow an egg so they would keep (very difficult with some of the smaller & thinner shelled ones like a Jenny Wren's), but even if you broke one you didn't go back to that same nest, even if it was a scarce one, we called it the Country Law.

Any-way, back to school one of the delights for me was the annual nativity play & I always had a part. Starting as a shepherd with a tea-towel round my head, then being Joseph at least twice! With a speaking part. One year we had something different & I played Old Father Time, alas my dad or mum, never got to see me in a play, but I am sure that's when the entertainment bug bit me! I loved listening to Children's Hour on the wireless when "Walking with Romany" was on, even though most of things that were done we already did! And also Wurzle Gummidge when we all used to copy his saying "stands to reason humans is daft" & few years later at a quarter to seven "Dick Barton Special Agent" when every night either Dick Barton, Snowy or Jock would be in dire straits at the end of each episode.

Eventually Hunningham School became just a junior school & the older pupils went to Leamington to Campion Secondary Modern if you didn't pass your 11 plus, Mrs Gilpin retired as there were only two classes. Not long afterwards Mr Helm also retired & moved into a flat in the village & we all helped him move. I was given an Oriental model of a bird made from nut shells from his house. Most would could go & visit him. This meant no new lads came camping but we still went on holiday with him. Miss Ellis then became Head teacher, looking back she had some guts following some-one like Mr Helm. But I think she did a good job for the rest of my time at Hunningham. (She still kept me as Head Boy) No more would we listen to the Derby & the Leger or some of the plays on the old radiogram in the classroom. We also used to listen to the News & Mr Churchill's speeches in awed silence during the war.

During the winter a lot of the lads started wearing Balaclavas (basically a large sock that you pulled over your head & it had a hole for your eyes, nose & sometimes your mouth) lots had been knitted by their mums In grey wool, some even had a bit of a peek above the eyes. I absolutely hated the things & thankfully my mum didn't knit she just did crochet, which meant I never had one well actually I just didn't like wearing a hat & still don't. Perhaps that's why I never became a bank robber! Ah that a bit unfair I suppose because I don't think any of the other lads ever robbed a bank either.

We did have fun on the way home gate vaulting or swinging on the gates & trying to walk along the top rail on the gated road but making sure they were shut afterwards most of the gates had a chain from the post to the

Gate with two old plough shares fixed to it which made them near enough self-closing! Or taking a bit of a detour to walk along the river bank looking for a pike, skimming stones or climbing the Willow & Wild Pear trees, trying not to rip our school clothes & listening for an Otter in the Willow roots

After school we would meet up & I am sure we looked like a motley crew but we did have fun rain or shine (it didn't seem to matter about getting wet then or when your hands got so cold you got "hot-aches"). We had great times in Oonagh's dads shed & with Eric & Julie first when they lived in the old Laundry at Flannel Reeves (their dad was in the army) playing all sorts of games by oil lamp. Making sure you closed a door carefully so the draught didn't break the lamp glass, lots of people put a hair grip on the glass as it was supposed to stop it breaking. When they moved to the house down the fields we had great times in the out buildings, particularly jumping out of the hay loft window onto a muck heap to see who could jump furthest (No matter how I tried I never won that one). We played all sorts of games in the hay bales & occasionally a bale would fall apart then we would attempt to tie it back together which was OK if it wasn't one of the old wire tied ones but we never tried to do any damage. Sometimes when playing in a cornfield that had just been cut a Stook would be knocked over as you wriggled into it, but you soon learned how to re-stook it in those days it was said that a Stook had to stand in a field long enough to hear the Sunday Church bells twice (which didn't work too well during the war as the Church Bells were not wrung, until 1942). When Flannel Reeves got a Combine for harvesting his corn (a tractor drawn one first) we had great times riding in the trailer full of corn & chasing the field mice, being careful not to get bitten. It was then we learnt if it was the right sort of wheat & you chewed it enough you made chewing gum which was OK but not as good as the Yankee sort. Eric's Dad had an old belt driven Motor Bike with a sidecar. Any way the sidecar body was removed & a door was fixed in its place, we seemed to acquire some petrol occasionally usually from Ray "as there as a bit left in the can after topping up the tractor". We had fantastic times riding round the field. Usually Eric drove (well it was his Dad's bike) & us others taking it in turns hanging on to the door. The more the old bike coughed & sputtered the better it seemed. I never knew what happened to that old bike or what happened when Eric's dad came home from the war! But the whole family moved away a few years later, I think back to Coventry & unfortunately we lost touch.

Peace

In 1945 on VE day we had a street party with tables in the road that seemed laden with food (where the food came from I will never know as it was rationed). The street was closed Mr Williams (who with his wife lodged at our house for a while & their oldest son Robert was born there) played music on a Radio gram & made a microphone out of an old earphone! A Barrel of Beer appeared (donated by The Plough I think) Everyone had a great time eating, singing & dancing with Scrogger, Fred, Alf & Ray dancing with the Land Girls (the married men including my Dad having to be careful with their wives around) We also had a bonfire in Greens Close (the field that made the square of Eathorpe). Next morning there were a lot of sore heads from the beer & a lot of rumbling stomachs from eating too much but my goodness it was worth it. The one part that was difficult for us kids was standing at the laden tables & being made to wait before we dived in while we remembered that our forces were still fighting the brutal Japanese at that time. We did celebrate VJ Day but the party was nowhere near as big or exciting as VE Day though really it should have been. Greens Close was where every year afterwards we started collecting wood during the summer holidays often using Flannel Reeve's horse & cart ready for Bonfire night. Now I think back he was brilliant to us kids, making sure there was no bull in that field when we were collecting wood & no cattle at bonfire night. We had a bonfire there & took our own fireworks or Crow Scarers which are fireworks on a rope & give a good bang. I know we weren't always sensible with the fireworks but I can only remember Jack getting her hair singed by blowing on a blue touch paper to make one go, & also a Jumping Jack following Shirley's Mum round her yard (they seemed to do that) she ran around & screamed but I'm sure just for us kid's entertainment. We had great times up until I was about 14 then a new person bought one of the thatched houses & complained so loudly about the risk of fire, we stopped. I remember once a young bull was put in Greens Close & unfortunately we used to torment it, by calling out near a fence then jumping over when it came running over. Then one of the others did the same the other side of the field I am now sure we ruined that bull! As ever after it had to wear a metal hood, so it had to hold its head up to see, which meant it couldn't lower its head to charge. Not one of our finest hours! There was a pond in the field right opposite our house & in the winter it froze over. What great times we had on that ice, even one year Alf (Choggie's oldest brother) even tried riding his motorbike on it. The amount of people who used to congregate on that pond, it's amazing we never went through the ice.

During the summer holidays a few of us would go to the Hall & pull weeds from the gravel on the front drive & for that Mrs Twist would give us homemade fruit flavour ice lollies! Yes she had a freezer. A big treat as that was the only place we could get them & if we weeded the tennis court we were allowed to try & play using some of her old racquets. I can never remember her paying us money.

It was about this time an Italian Family (alas I can't remember their name) that were living in a Caravan behind the pub in Marton started making Ice Cream & came round the area with a pony & trap selling it. It was much better than what we had in hospital & I think perhaps the best I've ever had. Not long afterwards the word was out we were going to have a mobile Fish & Chip lorry coming in the village, we were so excited to think Wow! Fish & Chips without going to

Leamington. When it duly arrived it was quite a big Van really with a fryer fitted that was coal fired (the fire was stoked from outside at the rear). Well I don't know whether the fat never got hot enough or what it was but the chips were like wet rag (worse than Mum's) I didn't try the fish but Dad said it was nearly raw. It was not long before that business venture went bang & we had to wait till we went to Leamington to Garibaldi's at the bottom of the town by the Railway bridge or Rugby for our Fish & Chip treat.

The Crossland brothers after leaving the army set up a factory by the Mill & started to repair & manufacture farm machinery. They fitted half-tracks to tractors & one machine I remember was a self-propelled potato harvester built round a Fordson Standard, which meant you didn't have to get serious back-ache picking up

Spuds. It was really impressive but not quite as successful as hoped because it was very heavy & when the ground was wet it got well & truly stuck. But they were very clever engineers & it meant broken parts could be welded, parts that the Blacksmith's Weld couldn't do.

Bob also returned to civvy street & lived in Rugby with his in-laws, he became workshop foreman at Rugby Portland Cement, working nights. I don't know whether it was Jimmy Malin's or the Army training but he was an absolute genius (OK I may be a bit biased) at making lorries & cars work, if he couldn't get a part he would make one. I remember a Wolsey sports car (Hornet I think) that needed a voltage regulator & as one was not available he made one out of an electric iron element.

Uncle Aubrey, Dad's younger brother started cycling from Rugby to Eathorpe after he was demobbed from the RAF, he never had a car either. He lived about two streets from

Grandad Goodwin, so we heard snippets of news & I said to Dad "one day I will take you to see him". I never met Dads elder Brother Vernon until Grandads Funeral, or his two sisters, one lived on the Channel Islands & the other had become a Nun & like Grandma Goodwin had died. I did meet Uncle Harold once, he suffered Shell Shock in WW1 & was in a Mental Hospital near Warwick & on one of the trips out they came to Eathorpe & I met him (what a terrible waste of a life, it showed there is nothing glorious in war) We did later meet Aubrey's wife (a truly lovely lady) & his four kids, Heh I had cousins. In the RAF he had been a Drum-major & an excellent Engineer, he was a wizard with a Mace, and it was at this time Majorettes were becoming popular from the USA & Aubrey spent a lot of time training these teams. Alas he died quite young with an enormous Brain Bleed.

Grandad was a retired Police Sargent from the Warwickshire constabulary, originally from Snitterfield near Stratford on Avon. The story was that he was very much the "Old Style Copper" & If there was any trouble in town he would go home, put on civvies & then go & sort out those who needed it (I think he told them they were naughty boys or something like that) you never messed with Sargent Goodwin. Grandma came from Southern Ireland & it was said she was a bit of a Firebrand, though I never met her

I think the Gran I knew died in 1946/47, I think losing two sons was just too much for her, so no more overnight stays at Newbold Road & trips to Rugby market where I loved hearing the "cheap jacks" getting a crowd round them as they were selling their wares & tried many times when on my one trying to copy their lines of chat

Learning the Job.

At this time there were lots of houses in the villages around Eathorpe that still hadn't got electricity. Dad being a qualified electrician quite often got the job of wiring the houses (back pocket money) at weekends & evenings in the summer. I often went along, Dad carried all his stuff on his bike, tools, wire, switches & plugs, & I would have a coil of wire on my handlebars that kept rubbing on the front tyre. I learnt how to lay cable flat with no kinks & to fix it with buckle clips, painfully learning how not to hit you finger & thumb with the hammer while holding a nail. About 5amp plugs & 15 amp plugs, about ceiling roses, junction boxes, switches & bulb holders, I learnt the basics of two-way switching & whether you used cable or flex. Also how to make plugs out of bits of wood to put in the rotten beams to hold the nails for the clips. In some of the old thatched cottages the timber was either rotten or full of wood worm, so you had to drill a hole & fill it with a new bit of wood. I also had a go at using a drift to drill holes in brick & stone but didn't like that much as it made your arms ache, because you hit the drift with a hammer the turned it a bit then did it again till you made a hole. I regularly got the job of going in the attic between the thatch & the ceiling when you could, amongst all the muck & bugs passing wire through holes. That's when you found the rat or mouse nest or worse the wasp nest I have always hated wasps I think they are the most Belligerent things on earth. There were so many places that got electricity thanks to Goodwin & Son. But because Dad was a bit soft, I know that there were some houses got wired for free because he wouldn't "chase his money". I must have learnt something about that as in later years I completely rewired my own house (when you were allowed to) & it all worked & still does. It was also then I learnt the difference between AC & DC current & why you would have to have huge cables to be able to have 240volt DC. I also learnt from Mr Williams (our neighbour) who was an excellent mechanic (nearly as good as Bob) how to Polarise & Energise Dynamos & Regulators, also how important Earth connections are on a vehicle, lessons "worth their weight in gold" later.

A lesson learnt

Shirley's brother Brian rented the field next to the coal yard & it also went between our gardens & the river, we always played football in this field, with the German prisoners of war. In Brian's field was also a tin shed by the Coal yard where if the weather was bad in winter (the river sometimes flooded part of the field) he could keep his stock indoors. He always had some mangolds & swedes to cut up for feed, cleaning the soil off with an old sheath knife. At that time I decided I really wanted a sheath knife & whenever we went by the Army & Navy store in Rugby or the Pawnbrokers in Regent's Street at Leamington Spa, I would look in the window & drool. Mum always said a definite NO. Well one day I stole Brian's old knife & tried to hide it at home. I'm sure you have guessed the outcome, Mum found it & demanded to know where it came from. I tried all the usual things about finding it etc., but eventually had to admit to stealing it. She made me even after loads of my pleading & even tears, go across the street to Brian's house, knock on the door & hand it back & say how sorry I was for stealing it. I just wanted to quietly take it back! Now, I don't pretend to be a Saint, but I can honestly say I have NOT stolen anything since then. (Except a bit of scrumping, but that's not real stealing is it?) I don't know whether it's the same now, but if I misbehaved Mum would say "you wait till your Dad gets home" well for me it was OK because he was more interested in the garden, his fags, the pub or fishing, so it was left to Mum to keep me in line anyway. She was not very big but when she gave you a clout you knew it. She didn't need a stick or a belt as her hand was more than adequate. I remember once in Leamington (it must have been before 1945) we were walking by the toy shop on Warwick Street, I think it was called Lentons? & there in the window was a model Sentry Box & I wanted it. Mum said NO so I started crying, then screaming, laying on the footpath & generally making a show, Mum gave me a whack on the bum & carried on walking toward the bus stop, after she had gone about 50 yards or more, I realized I wasn't winning so got up & ran after her saying how sorry I was. All that for something made out of Tate & Lyles Treacle Tins! And NO I never did it again, but I did get a Sentry Box sometime later but I never had a Sentry to put in it. Actually I know it's not the same now as you are not supposed to chastise kids any more. Well, all I know is it didn't do me any harm & I like to think it has kept me on the reasonably straight & narrow.

A lesson I learnt at about 15/16 was always check your pockets, for some reason Mum checked the inside pocket of my jacket & Loh & behold there was a "packet of three" (or Johnnies or Nodders or whatever you called them) in there. Which I had got just in case "I got lucky" (actually to make me feel big even though I knew they were more likely to get perished than used, because in those days the girls had a very good form of contraception it was a definite NO & a swipe across the cheek). Oh my G-d she went ballistic, suggesting I was committing every crime imaginable, when I tried to explain I was trying to be careful it didn't help much but eventually she did calm down & unbelievably replaced the packet in the pocket!

I also learnt not long afterwards something I should have known anyway & that was, that even a "backhander" round the ear from a big fella can "turn the lights out". George & I decided one evening to go to Stockton to check on the "talent", Mum always had a thing about George that he was trouble (perhaps she was right). We went on his motorbike &

after having a good look round we decided that perhaps there was better "talent" at Long Itchington, but as we got to the junction of the Southam Road for some reason he cut across the grass triangle, lost it & we finish up uninjured but covered in mud. That put the end of the "talent" hunt for that evening. When I got home there was a lorry parked outside our house, that meant Bob was at home & when I went in Mum said "What the Hell have you done" so I said we had come off George's Motorbike, she of course went ballistic at me for going with George & stupidly because sadly in your early teens you sometimes do these things, so I turned round & said "It's got nothing to do with you what I do" The next thing I knew I was picking myself up off the floor & hearing Bob saying "don't you ever speak to your Mother like that again". He had given me a real backhander & the "lights did go out" because he was a big fella, Ouch & I do mean Ouch.

Christmas time

I am writing this bit at nearly Christmas, my goodness how things have changed. Yes we did have Christmas & we always had a proper Christmas tree (where dad acquired them from I have no idea). The tree had little candles held in clips that were lit on Christmas day, later to be changed for a set of electric lights dad made at work with clear bulbs, twelve in a row painted different colours, that needed repainting every year as the paint used to peel off after a while.

I can only remember going to see Father Christmas in a shop once & that was at Bobbys on the Parade at Leamington. Bobbys was a shop Mum hardly ever went in as she said it was too dear & it was one of those shops that used capsules & vacuum tubes to pay for your goods, cor that fascinated me. Anyway I expect Mum must have had her Divi from the electric meter so she took me to see Father Christmas. Wow he sat on a big chair that was lit by fairy lights in a corner, with two Elves & a big sack full of parcels, he asked my name, if I had been good & what I was hoping for him to bring me on Christmas morning (I have forgotten my answer) but he gave me a present all wrapped up which I soon opened once we were out of the store & it was Snakes & Ladders & Blow Football (a little cardboard tube, a little ball & a goal frame). Not too exciting but at least I had seen Father Christmas & seen those things zinging around when someone bought something.

Presents were usually a book, a game (snakes & ladders etc.) an apple & some nuts. One year I had a wooden Fort. Joe (who Margaret was courting) bought me some lead soldiers. Another year I had a Farm with animals. One year my Dad made me an Electro-magnet at work & I played for hours picking things up the only problem being to put them down I had to switch it off at the plug! (Though dad was an electrician we hardly ever had a plug on the end of the lead, so the wires were held in the socket with matchsticks & yes we did occasionally get an electric shock). During the war Dad got a German prisoner of war to make me a dancing doll, that to make it dance you held the board between your knees, tapped the board & the doll danced.

At the end of the war Bob (my brother) had a wooden tank, just like the ones he worked on, made for me (I treasured that). I never had any cars to play with & I was always jealous of David who had Dinky toys, his mum & sisters were friendly with the Yanks & they got the Dinky toys. Some-times he would let me have a play with the odd car, but never the car & caravan! As I got older I got into Meccano (why was it you always lost the nut you needed to make that special tractor?) & Margaret & Nina often bought me a bit more for Christmas or birthday so I finished up with quite a collection & I made all sorts of things but mostly tractors or lorries & windmills.

That was a winter

It was now 1947 the year of perhaps the worst winter on record. We were cut off in Eathorpe first by snow that covered the hedgerows & meant that not only could we not get to school but people like my dad, who worked out of the Hamlet couldn't get to work. Finally Dad & others got out by going on a roundabout route through the fields. When the snow finally thawed which was much to our disgust as we had a brilliant sledging slope behind Choggies house next to The Plough. Where whenever there was snow our sledges would come out, these were a sheet of corrugated tin with two oak fencing rails nailed on as runners or just bits of wood nailed together no-one had a bought one, how we never got seriously hurt I'll never know. Not only as you had to bail out, at the end of every run because you had either a fence or a wall in front of you, but those bits of tin were sharp! The only casualty was Ray who one evening didn't bail out & hit his head a lot of blood but his mum patched him up.

Next there were major floods so still no way out, by then Flannel Reeves had bought an ex US army four wheel drive truck & used it to get people out of Eathorpe to work. To top it all there was then a major gale which brought down trees blocking roads as there were lots of big elm trees, before Dutch elm disease wiped the remainder out. No-one was short of firewood then. I remember dad going to Rugby once the road was open to get a new axe & saw to cut our logs. We had good fires at home for ages after that gale & plenty of wood ash to spread on the garden as fertilizer.

To get to school for the 11plus exam we had a taxi supplied that had chains on its tyres, because there were still no buses & the gated road was in a real mess. On arrival we were met by Mrs Somerton, who wanted to know why we hadn't been to school for eight weeks. We said we couldn't get there, her reply was "Where there's a will, there's a way" she somehow had got from Radford Semele to Hunningham nearly every day! Oonagh, Jack (Jaqueline) & Jill went to Princethorpe as they were Catholic. Julie & Eric also went to Hunningham School when they moved to Eathorpe. Because Eric lived down the fields & could still not get to the road he had to sit his exam a week later, Julie had done hers the year before, the same time as Shirley passed her 11plus, it was said that Julie had also passed but her parents decided against Grammar School.

Then came the results & from Hunningham that year Brenda & Gillian (who was born on the same day as me) who lived in Hunningham & didn't miss a day through snow etc. & I passed our 11plus, Oonagh & Jack also passed theirs. Hunningham & Princethorpe though being small schools always did well with 11plus.

Not long after those floods the River Leam by the marsh field was dredged by a Dragline by the War Agg I think, Cor we spent ages watching that machine dragging mud & rushes out of the river & spreading them on the bank. There was also a big punt that was used for trimming & cutting down some of the Willow trees. Obviously when the two workmen had gone home we had to try it out & had great fun with it but was always careful to put it back near enough where we got it from. We also had great times poking round the fires where they had been burning the Willow because if we put another piece on the embers it would not only burst into flames but also would crackle & sputter showering sparks, hence why you never used Willow on the fire at home.

Scary & expensive times

Now came the interview at the Leamington College for Boys, that was scary seeing the Head master in his black gown (I had never seen anything like that)! You were asked what books you liked to read (Treasure Island & Bird Books, if you did sport & a couple of maths questions. Any-way I was accepted, so I must have answered some of the Headmaster's questions correctly. So it was now time to get kitted out, the Green Blazer, Grey long Trousers, Green Cap (I truly hated wearing a cap) & School Tie could only be bought from the school shop on the premises & were expensive which gave Mum & Dad a shock but I am sure my sisters helped out. White Shirts (I didn't like the fact my shirts had loose collars so I had to have studs like an old man, why I had that sort I will never know, though perhaps because they could be bought second hand), Grey Socks & Black Shoes lace ups with leather soles could be bought where you could get them. I needed Gym Clothes & Plimsolls, Rugby Shirt, the colour of which depended on your house mine was green, for Jephson, Black Shorts, Socks & Rugby Boots (Soccer seemed to be a dirty word & was NOT allowed & you had to get permission to even play in a proper village team). I also needed a Satchel, (no such things as rucksacks then) so Dad got me a really good leather one at the same time as he got my Rugby boots from Gilberts at Rugby, where the Rugby balls were made. Luckily every year just after Christmas dad received a good bonus from the Lockheed & I am sure that's what kitted me out, though I think Nina & Margaret helped with the Blazer etc. In 1947/48 clothes were still very difficult to come by, so it must have a nightmare for all parents then whether you had the money & coupons or not. It did feel good having new clothes bought for me, as most of my clothes before, had been bought from a shop in Leamington, called Barbara Morris's Second Hand Clothes, (I don't think charity shops had been invented then), but I'm sure I was certainly not the only one, though I was at times so envious of some of the others.

Oh how things changed

There were so many changes going on at this time, voices had broken, I was going to wear long trousers soon & our games were changing too, no more would we be playing postman's knock or sardines etc., as the girls who were definitely growing up, had obviously all had serious lectures by their parents, as us boys had also. Dad always seemed to have an alleged old saying for anything & I remember he said to me at that time, "remember little fields have big gates" & one I thought was a bit rude! "If you want to be safe always drop it where you can see it" I thought years later that as good from someone who had to get married & had four kids. Though I am sure we all thought, we knew all there was to know anyway! Oh well, it was really good while it lasted! & Jill & I were still Boy & Girl-Friend on & off & when we were off I used to go up to Wappenbury Hill to Doreen's on a Saturday night & listen to the radio (Victor Silvester & his Slow Slow Quick Quick Slow, & when Comedy was King, ITMA with Tommy Handley, Much Binding in the Marsh with Jimmy Edwards, The Crazy Gang, The Goon Show & Have a go with Wilfred Pickles, a quiz program with the catch phrase "give 'em the money Barney & Carl Levis Discoveries) with her two brothers when her Mum & Dad were at The Plough, when the accumulator had been charged. The room always seemed warm when the paraffin lamp was lit, but care with the door! I had some very interesting experiences when the boys had gone to bed!

About that time if we had got a useable bike, we started going further afield, about five miles & anyone who hadn't got a bike we would give them a ride on the cross-bar (known as having a crossy), made it damned hard work but you helped a mate male or female. Always going to Long Itchington Wake Fair which was held on the village green & Southam Mop that was held just one night on the main road!, usually with no or very little money because there was no pocket money then. Though we did earn a little bit in the autumn, collecting Rose Hips, then taking them to Mrs Woodhouse who collected them for the WRVS, to be made into Rose Hip Syrup. We did get some rides by hook or by crook! The lights, the music, the atmosphere & the smell of hot oil was something special. There was also the attraction of some different girls to very clumsily try to chat up! Usually unsuccessfully. We would also go to Ufton or Marton when a Motor bike scramble was held. As we often had no real brakes on our bikes a groove was worn in the sole of our shoe where you put it on the front tyre to slow you down coming down Ufton Hill. It was about this time that we got into cycle speedway making up bikes with a small front sprocket (if we could find one at the tip) & racing round a track we dug out in Mr Robson's Wood & at Burnthurst. We also raced in the shrubbery dodging trees & racing down the bit of the Fosse Way by Mr Pearson's house & then broadsiding round the triangle. How we never got impaled in the odd car etc. that used that road I'll never know but we didn't! But the sole of our left shoe was quickly worn out. The only injuries I can remember was Brenda fell off & the brake lever went in her groin which was a doctor job & I fell off onto the bottom of on old bottle & it stuck in the top of my arm, where lots of stuff like worms came out which we pushed back in & all I was left with was a hole & a lot of blood! It healed but it is still there.

We also had a go at building trollies out of four old pram wheels, three bits of wood & a seat of some sorts. The longest piece of wood had one piece that was the same length as the axle on what were to be the back wheels & the next piece was fixed with a bolt on the other end of the main bit the axles were fitted to their bits of wood with fencing staples (being careful not to split the wood). Whatever you were using for a seat was fitted, a piece of rope tied to each side of the front axle so you could steer with that with your feet & you had your trolley! We didn't stick with them for long because we had too many nasty bumps, bailing out at the last second, because we just couldn't stop the damn things, but it seemed a good idea at the time. Alf & Fred Choggies elder brothers) went one better making a bigger Trolley & fitting an old Jap (I think) engine that had been used to drive a vacuum pump for a milking machine on some farm that Alf had worked on (War Agg). The tyre was taken off one of the rear wheels & a belt fitted to the engine that was bolted (not nailed) by the seat. To start it you pushed like hell & eventually the engine spluttered into life & off Alf or Fred went, to stop it there was a bit of spring steel with rubber on the end that you pressed against the plug, which was fine if you were stationary but bumping across a field stopping was very hit & miss after a few hits it was decided that perhaps that wasn't too good either. But perhaps it was the forerunner to modern Go Carts.

Alf always had smart Motor-bikes Vincent I think & one night coming back from Napton with Fred on the back went over a hump back canal bridge a bit quick & left Fred sitting on the road! (Only a few bruises luckily) but alas Alf did lose part of his leg a while afterwards in a Motor-bike accident.

Proper Gypsies

We also in the winter called at the gipsy camp below where Fred lived at Hunningham Hill, every year a family called Nayley (I think that's how it was spelt) over wintered on a wide verge & sometimes another family camped on a flat wooded piece by the river. These were proper gypsies not "didycoys", living in barrel top waggons pulled by strong half legged coloured horses that grazed tethered on the side of the road. We spent many evenings by their camp fires, watching them making pegs, Mr Nayley cutting the tin cans into strips & Mrs Nayley & the kids shaping the ash or willow twigs for him to nail the strips on, snares were also made of wire with the ground pegs made of willow, that if you stripped the bark, they could be seen by moon light. Many, many times since then I have tried to set a snare (when you were allowed) but I NEVER caught a thing. One of the amazing things they did was to make Chrysanthemum flowers by shaving a piece of Hazel stick which I think they soaked in water first & then dipping the finished head in dye, how they managed to shave the wood that thin & keep it from breaking off was magical. I have seen those flowers once since growing up, about 70 years on & that was at the famous Widecombe Fair. There were two daughters about our age Margaret & Omi who was gorgeous, but we knew we had no chance as we were not Romany & they would not get involved with a "Gorgio". At that time Randolph Turpin (who was a world champion boxer) & his brothers lived & trained at Leamington Spa & Mr Nayley used to spar with them. So even though we fancied the girls, you watched your Ps & Qs when he was around.

In the spring they would pack the waggons & go to the Vale of Evesham to pick fruit then return in autumn to pick potatoes, Mrs Nayley & the kids doing most of that but Mr Nayley picked up the cash. One evening we were round the fire enjoying a brew & a bit of rabbit or hedgehog, when Mr Nayley came back on his old sit up & beg bike from a session at the pub he got in a real

Paddy & threw his coat on the fire, alas in the pocket was a lot of money, by the time the remains of the coat was rescued there was not much money left! Mrs Nayley & the children would walk round the area selling the flowers, "lucky heather" & pegs as well as also offering to tell you your fortune. Later the parking spot by the river was cleared & was added to the field, so the family that camped there never returned & the wide verge became a layby used for storing chippings but there was always room for the Nayley's & their horses that Mr Nayley shod himself for many more years. But even they eventually stopped coming to our part of the world. It was such a shame not to see the spectacle of the family moving with their Barrel Top waggon & horses. The only traveller that used to visit then was the odd Tramp (Milestone Inspector) who would do odd jobs for a cup of tea & a sandwich or a piece of cake & a Knife Sharpener on his bike. What a brilliant bit of kit that was! With a stand for the back wheel & a pulley that drove a stone on the cross bar driven by a belt when he pedalled.

Adventurers

Going off on our bikes was always a bit of an adventure, as the bikes were bits & pieces we had rescued from the tip at Stretton & usually had tyres that had got patches on the side walls where they had perished. The tubes were more patch than tube, & lights were something that were always missing, so if you were riding in the dark & lights came towards you, you jumped off smartish & made believe you were pushing your bike, in case it was the local policeman. He knew you had been riding it but always smiled after asking where you had been.

It was about this time that we started to have boy & girlfriends. Yes we had all been friends growing up but this was a bit different (I suppose Hormones were starting to work). At different times we were boy or girlfriend with pretty well every-body but the one I always went back to was Jill, in fact her mum used to joke we were like a married couple because we were always falling out. As Shirley was two years older, tall & very glamorous, she DID look good in a bathing costume, she always had older boy friends from away, instead of us slightly podgy local lads.

Finally the day came to leave Hunningham School, it was a very sad day, as all my mates were going to secondary modern (Eric failed his 11plus after taking it a week late), in fact at one time I wanted to go with them but was told "don't be silly you will have more chances in life after Grammar". We all went to our new schools on the same service bus, but it was not the same. We didn't get a penknife, handbag or a wallet anymore, but I still had my holiday in Llandudno & five more weeks to get ready for Leamington College for Boys

That was the end of perhaps the best part of my life.

Book Two
Just a Country Kid
Long trousers! I must be growing up
Leamington College for Boys (Grammar School)

Like every-one else getting off that bus & walking to my new school I felt scared. Luckily I knew three lads from Hunningham who also went to "the College" (Harold, Bill, & Jeff) as they used to come camping with Mr Helm. Harold was two years older than me & Bill & Jeff were three years older. Arriving at the imposing front door was nearly enough to make you run but you had to go through it. You were met by a Prefect (who looked really grown up & you learnt to fear) & taken into the dining hall & you then saw all the rest of the First Year mob. Two masters in Gowns came in & called out you name, then told you which of four houses you were in (me in Jephson), your school number (178) & your class 1P. In the first year there was no A or B grade just 1 & 1P. You were then introduced to your form Tutor (Capt. Fosse). You were then taken into the main hall & The Head Master entered from his office at the back & we all stood as he made his way to the stage, (he was not very big but he seemed more imposing now than when I had my interview perhaps it was the Mortarboard). He welcomed us & said that there was everything we needed at the College it was up to us to make use of it. After he had finished we all gave him some applause & he left via the main hall to the Holy of Holies (his office). It was then I became Goodwin, 178 Jephson instead of Roy & we were showed where our form-rooms were situated & the quickest way of getting there,

1P form room was on floor three, & our lockers were next to the tuck shop. We each found a desk & on each desk were books etc. that we would need to start with, the ink wells were full, as even though Biros were around then, we were not allowed to use them. By now it was mid-morning break time & time to go for a pee, finding the toilet in the middle of the room was a pedestal with a tap in it I didn't know what it was so I peed in it, later finding out it was a drinking water fountain!. Coming out of the toilet I was met by three or four second year lads who tried to take me back in the toilet to push my head down the pan & flush it (an old tradition) well I didn't think much to that & fought back. That caused a commotion, a master arrived & I was in trouble for fighting on my first day, I was given "lines "to do but didn't know what they meant so I had to ask one of the other kids (my G-d I felt a fool) but I never got "ducked".

Capt. Fosse was an Ex-Army Officer whose subject was German, he had been injured in the World War having a wound in his face which made him slur his words. Which we immediately picked up on & mimicked when he wasn't around. It did seen funny not having any girls there, I found out later the only females were the three in the kitchen & the Head-masters secretary. For the first few days we were shown where to go for each lesson & how long you had to get to that room. It was also the time to meet the masters who taught the different subjects. It seemed so weird that the Masters all wore black gowns with long sleeves, we were soon to learn that those long sleeves when laden with pieces of chalk could give you a smart whack round the head when swung by Mr Raucliffe (the Latin Master). It was also at this time I learnt that the eleven o'clock break was not "the Lunch break" that was known as Recess & was what I knew as "Dinner time" & "Dinner time" was actually what we called "Supper". Why doe's everything be so confusing at these times? One of the choices was French or German after meeting the French Master I decided the go with Capt. Fosse & try to learn German. The only real thing that has been useful to me from that was learning the original woods of "Silent Night" which a long time later I taught (frenetically) to a singing group & it went down well, whenever I went to Germany they spoke better English than me. The Physics Master (Mr Sutton) was an imposing figure with a booming voice, who we would soon learn was a brilliant shot with the wooden blackboard rubber if you were not paying attention he would say "What are you selling boy"& would confiscate anything he thought you shouldn't have (you usually got said item back at the end of the lesson). The Maths master Mr Onslowe (known as Pup because he did yap) was also the Deputy Head Master & he told us from day one that he had been teaching so long, that not to think we could come up with an excuse that he hadn't heard before, (but of course we tried). For Music & Religious Instruction we had Rev Saberton who I thought being a Vicar was going to be easy on us but I soon found out he didn't have a sense of humour (well, at least like mine) when I wrote a poem about Dr Faustus that I found really funny & so did the rest of the class, he didn't. That's when I learnt he was quite useful with an old violin bow (minus catgut) on the backside. Funnily enough that's when I realized I was not interested in Religion or his sort of music. We were introduced to Mr Kaufman the woodworking Master, as we were all allowed to do woodwork for the first year & then you could carry on if you were in a B stream while the A stream did Latin! I actually made a coffee table, which I never did take home, perhaps just as well because I am sure it would have fallen apart, after learning about saws & chisels but it taught me I would never be a carpenter. Unless I could use 6inch nails! The History

Master was Mr Taylor (spud) he also taught sport. The names of the Chemistry & Biology Masters & also the English Master for Language & Literature, escape me now (well it was seventy years ago!) We were also introduced to the scourge of all First, Second, Third, Fourth & Fifth year boys, "Prefects" who were all six formers usually on their way to university (that was before everyman & his dog went to university), they were next door to God & had gold on the edges of their blazers! They could & did dish out punishment usually "lines" or you had to clean up their rooms for anything that seemed to them to be misdemeanours. I very soon learnt that if you were seen out of school & you hadn't got your complete uniform on Blazer, White Shirt, and School Tie & Cap you were in trouble. I hated wearing a Cap so it cost me lots of 500 lines. Even in the summer you were expected to wear a Tie, but I remember one year we were allowed to undo the top button of your shirt, but that was no use to me with my bloody loose collars!

It was then I realised just how far behind most of us "country kids" were compared to a lot of the "town kids" we had never heard of Geometry, Algebra, Logarithms etc. we had just done Sums, we had never learnt science, except the bit of biology we learnt growing up, we had not learnt any French or German & certainly no Latin but there were quite a few lads who had been to private schools & had started them so who were way ahead to start with. But I knew they hadn't been to a better school than our little Hunningham.

One of the first things I learnt was if you were in class & you wanted to go to the toilet, you were usually told to wait until the end of that lesson. So if you had been given "Syrup of Figs" because you were "bunged up" it was advisable to take a note to give to the Master to say you had taken it, just to save an embarrassing accident.

Some of us "country kids" went to school by train, some by Stratford Blue buses (that came out of the ark) but most of us by "Midland Red". Alas the trains & the bus companies have long gone. One of our favourite games on the bus was as we were loading at Warwick Street on the way home, someone would open the rear safety door & we would walk down the bus jump out the back & run around to the front again, bloody annoying for the conductor, the buses were all half cabs & the odd one was petrol, that used to regularly boil.

It was at the College that I first tasted Whale meat Yuk! The Government decided because of meat shortages to try serving Whale meat & Reindeer meat to some schools as an experiment, & alas we were some of the Guinea Pigs. The Whale meat was just like squares of deep red rubber (G-d it was awful & I was just thankful that the rule about not leaving the table before your plate was empty didn't apply at the College or I reckon we would still be there). The Reindeer meat was just about OK, needless to say I have never tried either since but Venison is really nice. Another food disaster was when some girls came from another School for part of their "Domestic Science course & they made Custard & burnt it! There is very little worse than burnt Custard & it took me years before I would try it again.

I remember one English Literature class particularly as it was the day George Bernhard Shaw died, the Master was one of the younger ones & was a bit intense, he was totally heart-broken & I'm sure he would not have been more upset if George Bernhard Shaw had been his Dad (perhaps he was). The lesson really turned into chaos particularly when someone suggested that G B S had "Gone back to Methuselah"! That was a detention & nearly for the whole class, but it was damn clever, that's why I didn't think of it.

Once a year we would have Speech Day when all the masters would wear not only their gowns but also their silks & Mortar-boards, speeches would be given by the Headmaster, Head boy & a visitor Usually Sir Frank Whittle (an old boy who made the jet engine work). We were expected to listen for about three hours so if you had a copy of a comic to sell you could usually find someone who was sitting away from the aisle who you could sell it to. One year we had a Deep-sea Diver come & give us a talk with all his kit, now that was interesting & very exciting. After lunch there was a showing of the School Film in the Dining hall with clips from every year. The only time there was a School Photo was on one Speech Day & I was not allowed on it because I didn't have a fresh collar on my shirt, (I just didn't have a fresh collar they were all washed to death). I suppose they thought I was a bit of a scruff! & perhaps I was. So my image was never on a School Photo, but I can live with that.

St Tudno & a new Bike

About this time two lads from Coventry used to come to Eathorpe camping in the summer, camping at the side of the road past the river bridge by Kenning's field. On lad called Eggo (he became one of Shirley's boyfriends) I think his name was Eric built a canoe or perhaps a kayak out of a frame covered with canvas from old Ex-Navy kit bags & towed behind his bike on two pram wheels. After trying it out on the river he decided not to take it home. So Dick (Choggies brother) bought it. Dick was one of the few in the village who couldn't swim & after nearly drowning because he turned turtle & had a job getting out as the hole you sat in wasn't very big & then only saving himself by grabbing some reeds, so he decided to sell it & dad bought for me for 2quid. (Dick couldn't swim but he was brilliant on a bike & would ride over the waterfall & even the river bridge parapet, yes I know it was daft but he could do it). I don't know whether it was the shape or what but it did take some handling but somehow I took to it like a duck to water. I loved that boat, perhaps because I could do something no-one else appeared to be able to do, I even named it St Tudno. One year mums cousin from Stoke on Trent came for a week's holiday & as he was a painter & decorator I got him to paint it, he also painted St Tudno on both sides. I used to paddle from behind our house upstream to the Pool, where lots of people including adults tried to paddle it & all rolling over. We had a panic one day when one of the Crosland brothers had a go & he was really tall, when it rolled over he couldn't get out & it took a lot of help to get him out spluttering & vowing never to try again. I really don't know why I never had any problem with it but I suppose to show off a bit. I used to take it to Grove Pool & get the others to try & tip me out by jumping in by me, OK very stupid but I never ever turned turtle. Occasionally I would paddle from home up stream all the way to Robsons on a Sunday for afternoon milking then paddle home, it was a long way!

I was also given an EX RAF big eight man rubber dinghy with some German WW2 paddles. We used to paddle it upstream (that was real hard work) up to the Pool where we had great time jumping in & out of it. We used for years even when it got a bit rotten & started to leak. But alas one night when the river flooded & I had left it in the field, instead of struggling over the fence it was washed away & trashed. So that was the end of that, but I still had St Tudno.

For my 13th Birthday Dad decided I needed a new bike (I suppose he had a good bonus that year) I had a morning off milking we walked to Princethorpe & caught the bus to Rugby. There was one shop that Dad said had been there when he was young so was the best so that's where we went, after looking at so many bikes he bought a red one with drop handlebars, white mudguards & Derralia? Gears. Wow was I chuffed & to get it home I rode the bike along some roads I had never seen, Through Bilton, Dunchurch, the A45 & going full pelt along the" straight mile" then having a breather before the next bit. I soon showed every one my new bike & of course used it to go milking the next morning. It didn't take too long before the mudguards came off & straight handlebars were fitted (much to Dad's disgust) to make it much easier to use it on the track in the shrubbery & round the Island by Pearsons.

Gym & Sports

The very first Gym lesson we had in the very smart Gymnasium taught me I would never be a gymnast! There was a lot of difference between climbing & hanging from trees to doing it from proper equipment. I could do handstands (to a fashion) but I could not do forward or backward rolls properly & flips were definitely a no go. I could climb trees but I never could climb a rope (still can't). That first time with us all together in the changing room also made me realise I was the only one who didn't wear underpants (no I don't know why perhaps because dad didn't).

To get to the sports field we had to go along-side the Brewery opposite the rear gate of the College, it was there we stood in our new Rugby kit & Spud Taylor explained how you SHOULD play it & tried to instil in our heads some of the rules, divided us into two teams (there were thirty one in each class) & we had a go. It was decided I should be Hooker so I was taught how & when to hook the ball to the back of the scrum. I soon learnt that if I didn't get the opposing hooker's shins he would get mine, if the ref wasn't looking of course. I quite liked Rugby, which was just as well as we were not allowed to play soccer. If you were a member of a village or town side you MAY have got a dispensation. Swimming was my thing & I was perhaps better at that than any other sport. For a while I was the best at free-style for my year, then a new boy arrived & no matter how I tried (I got disqualified once for turning on the bar instead of the wall & I still didn't beat him) I remember at one Gala the Mayor was giving the prizes(Certificates) & I came second & when my name was announced he said obviously trying to be funny" It's a pity you didn't win as it would have been a goodwin", I did try to smile but wanted to punch him (not just for his crap humour but also because I wanted to win). I took up Life-saving & was chuffed to bits with my medals (hopefully my son still has them). What training we had for Galas & Lifesaving was very little & far between because there being only one swimming bath in Royal (I quite often miss that bit) Leamington Spa was shared by all schools & public. We were trained by the Indomitable Mrs Cross, who though she was quite small had one hell of a voice (its funny how sound amplifies in a swimming pool). It meant that whatever she told you to do you tried to do it, because you didn't want her to yell louder Actually I had an advantage in the summer because I had Eathorpe pool to train in! Which was just as well because if the training was after school I couldn't do it. I remember one inter house Swimming Gala when Jephson was looking for a diver, one lad said he would do it, I don't know whether he was just brave or at the Gala forgot how to dive off a quite high board but he took off & did the biggest belly-flop ever. Masters & Mrs Cross all rushed to get him out of the pool but luckily all he suffered was a very, very red belly & a hurt pride. Perhaps it helped that he had got quite a bit of fat there. I used to dive off the pillars at the Eathorpe pool but that diving board was a bit high to dive from for me though I didn't mind jumping from it. Running, particularly sprinting I was rubbish at but cross-country though I hated it I was not too bad at but never a winner. It was always difficult for me with after school hours sport because if I missed the bus home it meant walking. So even if I was good enough to be picked for something sometimes it was not a good idea. I did play Rugby for my house & three times for the school in the Intermediates. I remember one Saturday going by coaches to Rugby to play against Lawrence Sherriff School. When we arrived we thought we had got the wrong opponents, they were huge & they ran rings around us & through us, we were stuffed. The seniors who had also been playing were stuffed too. On each coach there were players from both teams & on the way home some of the senior lads started sing rather mucky songs & it seemed lovely to all be like mates. Alas on Monday when I spoke to one of the Prefects that had been on the coach like a mate, it meant I had a load of lines to do (a Lesson learnt). What happens out of school does not happen in school. Cricket I was not very good at & Tennis though we had proper Tennis Courts I never did play at school because that was an "after-school activity" So to say I was a star at sport would be pushing it a bit but I did alright.

Entertaining again

After a few weeks the Arts Master (whose name I have forgotten) decided we should make some Glove Puppets after first considering Marionettes, then deciding we would have all sorts of trouble with all those strings. So if the Glove Puppet idea worked we would put on a show like Punch & Judy but as The Swan Lake. So we all got busy making Paper-Masse heads, my head was good enough to be the Princess! & our mums were asked to make costumes. (Bit challenging for me knowing my mums sewing skills). But anyway it turned out alright. So we started rehearsing & in one of scenes the puppets were Waltzing. I am sure that most people have seen a Punch & Judy Booth, can you imagine two lads with a puppet on one hand above their hands twisting & turning & then exiting the back quick to let two more in! It took us ages to learn not to titter or swear when you got it wrong & still remember what few words you had. Finally it did work & we did a show for the school, even though it went down well, those of us in it took some stick. We did the same show one evening in the Loft Theatre, & it went brilliantly. As it was in the evening I stayed with one of my school friends at Emscote, Snooty Harris whose dad worked with mine. It seemed so funny sleeping in a room that had a street lamp right outside the window & an upstairs Bath-room & toilet. We didn't have any of those things in Eathorpe. It was so good to be again in a school play, even if I was only using one hand.

At home in the living room at both sides of the chimney breast there was an alcove, in the right hand one was the Radiogram (the one from Grans), so I decided I would make the other into my Punch & Judy Booth, with a couple of old sheets & a piece of wood. With my wood working skills getting the piece of wood the right length & then to stay in place was quite an exercise. After quite some time with Mum getting a bit fed up with trying to make costumes & me making a mess with Paper Masse & paint I had a few characters. I had already written my script, so all I needed now was an audience, so I invited all the kids in the village. Luckily they didn't all turn up but those who did had a good laugh, with me attempting to do different voices, because the show was all about Mr & Mrs Woodhouse (Woodlouse). Dad said it was wrong to be so rude (even though he wasn't there, he was at the pub), but Mum laughed at it. That was not the last time Roy & his puppets performed there. Perhaps the best performance was by one of our resident mice, when it decided to run up the corner of the Alcove into the hole that had been there for years, during my show. The screams, mostly from the girls & the laughter, made me think I was really good that night, till I was told the truth. Fancy on your way to stardom being up-staged by a mouse.

There is more than School

During my second year at Leamington College for Boys, Mum & Dad decided I ought to get a part time job. There certainly weren't any paper-rounds so I was found a Saturday & Sunday job helping milking cows & odd jobs at Mr Robsons farm. The farm was on the old carriage drive to Marton so I knew where it was. For helping with the milking I would receive 11shillings, Yippee I was going to be rich! Well perhaps not as 2shillings & 1 penny went to School dinners (no I could never understand the extra penny either) & any clothes I needed I had to buy. And by then I had got a taste for the odd Mars bar or two which at the time cost 3pence each.

I asked Mum to get me a pair of EX Army boots from the shop in Regent Street next time she went to Leamington I had a bit of money from Rose Hips & she added the rest, well she couldn't find my size so bought me one size bigger which meant wearing two pairs of socks (which wasn't too bad as long as the outside pair didn't run down & rub you toes) but at least I had a pair of Hob Nail Boots even if they were second hand!

In those days on the farm the Cowman did the milking, the Waggoner looked after the horses & sometimes drove the tractor & the general farmworker did most things but was not paid so much.

The first morning I was so keen to be at work on time at 6 30, I set my alarm & somehow got it wrong, because when I got to the farm on my old bike there was no sign of life, after hanging around a bit I decided to go home & got a puncture on the way. When I got home & checked the clock on the mantelpiece it was still only 5 30 so I don't know what time I started my original trip. Instead of trying to repair the puncture I decided I would walk. So at 6 o'clock off I went walking through the woods I had this feeling something or someone was following me. I tried talking with a gruff voice & when I looked round quickly & saw a fox, that when I shouted ran away, but to this very day just to see a fox makes my hair on the back of my neck stand up just like a dogs hackles. When I arrived at the farm there were lights on & the cows were just being brought from the covered yard to the milk parlour, I met first Dai the Cowman & then Mr Robson & his Graham they told me what to do (mostly shovelling & sweeping cow sh dung) but as the weeks went on I learnt more & more & enjoyed it. As I had tried milking goats, at least I had some idea, what to do when I was asked to have a go at milking, a squirt from each cow before the milking machine was put on the teat, to check for Mastitis! (Oh yes I was learning). I soon learned the names of most the cows & knew how much protein feed to give each one by pulling the lever on the hopper. The amount was worked out (not by me) by how much milk they were giving. I also learnt how to judge & set the flow of the milk over the cooler to get the temperature right & also to make sure you kept your eyes on the milk churn so it didn't overflow, but I still shovelled ---- dung!. After milking the others would go for breakfast but I would then start getting bails of straw & put new bedding in the covered yard. I also learnt about the Warble Fly that laid its eggs in a cow's skin, the eggs then turned into a huge grub under the skin on the cows back, you could see the lump or lumps on its back. When the grub was ready to emerge a hole would appear, we would then squeeze the grub out & kill it, they were disgusting, to keep the Warble Fly at bay we used to rub Jeyes Fluid over the cows back & it helped. Once a cow had a problem with Warble Fly, its hide was of no use for leather as it had holes in it.

It was not too long before it was suggested that I used the horse & cart, the were two horses in use & the Waggoner (I think it was Jack, but remember he only had one eye after losing one to a Blackthorn bush, & lived in a house across the fields the other side of the carriage drive) decided I ought to use the smaller one. I said I knew how to put the harness on (well I'd seen the harness on Dolly, Flannel Reeve's horse) Not being very tall it took ages for me to put the collar on, that damned horse was not going to make it easy for me & turn it, then the bridle, that horse by then knew I didn't know much & refused to open its mouth for ages to get the bit in. Then came the saddle & breaching, after a couple of attempts I got the saddle on its back & then tried to work out how to put on the breaching. Because as I had dropped the saddle a couple of times the breaching was all tangled up. I knew one piece went round the horses dock but to get that there, I started to undo buckles! I did finally get that horse ready for work but I know it was really fed up before I had finished & it says something about its temperament that it put up with me. Obviously the Waggoner had a darned good laugh at my expense but perhaps it taught me that I didn't know Everything about Anything. But once that horse was in the cart I was quite proud of myself.

One of the first jobs each morning in spring & summer was to get the horses out of the field in front of the house & into the stable, in the winter they stayed in overnight. But at least once a year as you drove them to the stable they would have a mad five minutes a run amok over the lawn & churn it up! If I happened to be there on that day it was a job for "the boy" to put the turf back & pull the roller over it. As the Boy you got all the odd jobs I remember being sent with a spade to slice off the Ant-hills on one the fields, after slicing them off you had to chop them up & spread them G-d that was an awful job for a 13year old but not quite as bad as spreading muck all on your own. Muck was loaded from the covered yard or muck heap into a cart then taken to the field then dragged out in heaps about 10 yards apart later to be spread, (why it wasn't spread straight from the cart I'll never know). Afternoon milking time could not come round soon enough on those days. Perhaps the best Saturday ever was when it was decided I could drive the tractor! A Standard Fordson that ran on Petrol\Paraffin starting on Petrol then when the engine was hot switching to Paraffin (TVO) I was going to Scuffle a field over the Carriage Drive. I was shown how to start the tractor by swinging the handle (hard work) making sure my thumb was not round the handle in case it kicked back (if it did you could break your thumb). Well after quite a few swings, well pulls really because you pulled the handle upwards, it coughed & burst into life, Wow it was then I learnt that when you parked up the Fordson at night you always clipped the clutch\brake pedal down not just for the brake but because it was a "wet" clutch it could take you 15 minutes to get it in gear. So off I go out of the yard with scuffle hooked on behind & half way across a grass field I stopped & switched over to Paraffin as I had been told, started off again & somehow pulled the rope that dropped the scuffle, the tines ripped into the grass & stalled the tractor. Because I had just switched to Paraffin the bloody thing would not start, so I had the walk of shame back to the farm-yard to get help. Petrol \ Paraffin engines are notoriously bad for starting when warm. I got one hell of a telling off & was made to replace the turf but was allowed to do my driving job once the tractor had been started (a serious lesson learned). I felt like a King going up & down that field. Luckily it was not the last time I drove that tractor & I loved it. During Hay, Silage & Harvest time during school holidays I did all sorts of jobs mostly with a fork, but I earned a few bob. That bought a new shirt with collar attached for College.

Enough to pay for my week's holiday with Mr Helm & when I was 14 I bought my first motor-bike! A very ancient BSA Sloper that had been stripped of mudguards & lights because someone had tried to make it into a "track bike". Well it was a big old thing, a side valve 500 cc with a total loss oil system, but it ran. I walked all the way to Burnthurst paid my 2 quid & rode it home stopping at Wappenbury garage to put in half a gallon of petrol for one shilling & four pence. Mother went ballistic when I got home but she got used to me tinkering with the thing in the back yard. I know I was too young to ride on the road, it had no number plates (never did know what the Reg number was) & it was not taxed or insured but you did daft things then & luckily got away with them.

On Sunday mornings after milking I would bike to Hunningham & join some of the other lads & men from round the area for a game of football, the pitch was in a field by the pub next to the Cricket Field & by the river. There were goal posts but the rest was guess work. There were always plenty of cow pats to step or slide in & a throw in was when the ball went in the river or over the hedge the other side. Some had football boots & some used work boots, George from Offchurch only had work boots but he was a brilliant player who could run rings round most of us. Joe & his brother Cyril (a Wolves fan) always came after they had finished milking & quite a lot there were to do with farming. We usually had enough for two good sides, I usually played in goal. One of my claims to fame, was that I would, when needed run out of the goal & dive on the ball at the player's feet. If that player was Joe, as quite often it was, he would always say" Bugger you Gudgeon". We had so many great times with knocks & scrapes but they were worth it, whenever the ball went in the river & couldn't be reached it was always Gudgeon (me) who took their shirt off & went in the river no matter what time of year. (OK I don't know why I took my shirt off perhaps it shows I was daft even then). After the game the older ones would have a pint & us others a Vimto if we had enough money though quite often the older lads bought us a drink.

Air Guns.

Not sure whether I was 14 or 15 years old when I first got interested in Air Guns. One of Choggie's older brothers bought a Webley 177 Air Pistol & quickly showed it off to us. (He also had a 4.10 Shot Gun but couldn't get any Cartridges for that). Wow this was something & when he let us have a go with it (trying to hit a tin can on a post) cor I loved it. Even though I missed the can I did hit the post once. The Webley was quite heavy & I needed two hands to fire the thing. Anyway I decided I wanted an Air Gun, after finding out the price of a Webley (even second hand) I looked round for something that suited the size of my pocket. I found an Air Pistol called a Gatt that was quite cheap, so I went to the Army & Navy Store at Rugby & bought one along with a box of pellets. To load the Gatt you removed a screw that had a short probe on the end from the rear of the barrel, put a pellet in the hole then push the pellet into the chamber with the screw to tighten, to cock it you push the muzzle on a hard surface until it went right in the barrel & locked. As you fired it the action of the muzzle flying forward propelled the pellet. Well it worked but the action of the muzzle flying forward made its accuracy very questionable though not as bad as the rifles at the Fair.

We were fooling around one evening by Mr Pearson's house that had the end wall covered in Ivy, the Webley was fired at something in the Ivy, the Pellet ricocheted off the wall & stuck in Dick's ear, and Oh my G-d there was a panic! Luckily the Pellet or part of it only just bruised the skin & didn't break the surface. Even though we did daft things we never ever shot into that Ivy again. After a while I got fed up with the Gatt & Dick had a Diana Air Rifle that he said he would swap for the Gatt, so I became the owner of a Diana. Well what a heap of junk that was! No wonder he wanted to swap, it was so lacking in power I'm sure you could see the Pellet come out of the barrel, but I was so determined not to let him know that he had got one over on me I never said a word. I carried on using the Rifle for quite a while but I always put it down to it being no good when I couldn't hit a damn thing.

For my 15th Birthday Dad decided (against Mothers wishes) to buy m a decent Air Rifle so he went to Rugby to the same shop he bought my Bike from & bought me a BSA Cadet Major 177 Air Rifle. When I saw it I thought all my Birthdays & Christmases had come at once. Wow this was a proper gun & I couldn't wait to show it off! Everybody wanted to have a go & they were all saying how good it was I felt about Eight Feet Tall, I must admit though I could now hit the tin can I was never going to be a Buffalo Bill or Annie Oakley but I had great time trying. We used to go Rabbit hunting but I never hit one & when we were Grey Squirrel hunting I used to shoot into the Dray & one of the others shot the Squirrel (which was worth a Shilling from the War Agg).

I kept that Rifle for many years even when the newness wore off but was never ever a good shot, oh my G-d how many more things was I no good at?

Show Business

One Saturday Mr Robson asked me if I would like to go to Kenilworth Show that was on the next Saturday, as they were going to show two cows & a Bull that they had been halter training. Their herd were Dairy Shorthorns a breed that was very popular in Warwickshire. Of course I said "Yes please" I had only been to Kenilworth once before & that was to see the ruined Castle.

It was decided Graham was going to stay home to do the afternoon milking, the two cows would not be milked in the morning so their Udders looked good & then all three animals would be washed before loading in the cattle truck. The day arrived & I was there at 6-30 as usual, this time I was helping Dai to wash the white bull & to give the two Roan coloured cows a really good going over. The truck arrived & everything was loaded quite easily Dai was going in the truck & I was going with Mr & Mrs Robson, their younger son Gordon (who always said he was going to be a famous inventor & perhaps he did) & their Daughter who's name escapes me (she was about two years older than me & Dai used to tease her regularly & I think she enjoyed the attention). We arrived at the showground a bit after the truck & the animals were unloaded, Dai had started washing them again & I was sent to help. Little did I know that I would be doing that all bloody day! The white bull had a habit of when he went to the loo he swung his tail covering the back end of his body in sh-t. I thought I was going to have a day out but I never got away from the cattle lines & to top it all I was bitten for the first time but alas not the last by a Horse-fly on my cheek & it bled for ages, they are evil little buggers. We didn't win any prizes & ironically most of the Cups were won by Joe Kenning's family. But I NEVER offered to go showing again!

In 1950, I think it was, the local WI decided to enter a Festival of Short Plays at Royal Leamington Spa (see gave it full title) & it was decided to give a performance of the two plays in one of Flannel Reeves's barns as Mrs Reeves was the local President. I think it was a lady who had moved into the cottage two doors from us with her husband & daughter, who came up with the idea as she was into dramatics (it was her husband who had been in the RAF who gave me the dingy) So the barn was cleared & a bit of a stage was built & bales were put in place for seating. One of the plays was called "Rory aforesaid "(or something like that) & was set round a fire. In one part some-one was stabbed in the chest. The climax being when someone put a Cross on the fire & there is a big flash. Dad being the electrician of the village was asked to come up with something. The fire bit was just a red bulb, but the flash was a bit different. After a bit of thought he came up with the idea a square wooden base with two steel pins sticking up a positive wire fixed to one & negative to the other a strand of thin fuse wire fixed between them, a small bit of flash powder was placed under the wire. The cable fixed to the pins was connected to a switch & plugged into the power. The idea being as you switched on the fuse melted dropped onto the powder & proof, do you know what it worked, with a big flash & smoke the WI & the audience were delighted. There was also a wind machine which I don't know if it was borrowed or someone made it. It was a small barrel with slats fixed across it & a piece of canvas covering it in a frame with a handle, as you turned the handle & the slats rubbed on the canvas it sounded like wind! (Well, if you turned the handle at the right speed)

When it came to the Festival Saturday Dad couldn't go, so I had a day off milking & took his place because I knew what to do (allegedly). The Festival was held in the Church Rooms at the rear of the building where the Spa Water Fountain was housed (for those who have never tasted that Spa water, it tasted worse than sea water but was supposed to do you good). I was given a lift to Leamington with the wire etc. & someone else brought the wind machine. There was a proper stage with curtains & loads of seats, when we arrived I thought I ought to try out the flash to make sure I had got it right & wow it worked. It then came to our turn to perform, everything was set up rather quickly as you were timed & away we went, with me turning the handle in the wings & the wind sounding OK, when the actor was stabbed he put his hands to his chest & there was blood! I couldn't believe what I just saw & to be honest expected him to die (It was not until afterwards that I was shown how it was done. In those days you could buy petrol for Cigarette Lighters in Rubber Phials that you pierced the tip & squeezed the fuel into the lighter, well a file was emptied & carefully some red poster paint was sucked into the Phial, it was then taped to the actors palm & when he put his hand to his chest he squeezed out the paint, very clever & realistic, they didn't do that bit at Eathorpe) At the end of the play, the actor put the Cross on the fire I flicked the switch & nothing!! The actor had put the Cross on the fire & it had fallen across the fuse wire & broken it, so no flash. The adjudicator on summing up said the play was good but one of the effects let them down, G-d I have never been so embarrassed in my life. Even though everyone realised it was not my fault, but Heh that's what's known as Show Business.

Graham & I started going to Brandon Speedway on a Saturday night by mini bus, we had great nights watching The Bees when Bob Fletcher was skipper. The sound of those JAP engine with no silencers & the smell of Castrol R (Joe always said "he could fry his bacon in that stuff") was so exciting, there were always big crowds & everyone stayed for the "learners races" at the end of each meeting if only to see them fall of. The Speedway trips took all my money but it was worth it.

I was enjoying working at Robsons but enjoying school less by the week, I was finding it hard to keep up with Grammar School routine (homework etc.) even though I always stayed in the A class & having to earn my own money, so when I reached 15 I had a serious talk with Mum & Dad about leaving school, even though I was supposed to stay until 16 at least. Anyway it was decided against my sister's wishes that I should apply to leave School early. I collected the form from the Secretary, got it filled in & Mum & I had to see the Headmaster. After much Humming & Haaaing he decided, to use his words "I would perhaps make a better farmer than a scholar" & signed the form. Well, not everybody wants to be a Scientist or some fancy Engineer & after being bored stiff by hearing on Speech Days both types of people talking about what they did, I certainly didn't even though I knew they earned more money than perhaps I never would.

I left Leamington College for Boys on Maundy Thursday 1951 never ever to return.

Jill & I were still on & off boy & girlfriend & now her Dad had got a Television! & Speedway was shown on it so I was invited to go & watch it, & her mother always said "I see you have come to see Jill again" & made us sit together, we would nearly always fall out before the evening was through.

I do have some regrets in my life & perhaps the biggest was when Jill died in a cycling accident on her way home from work at Ryton in 1953/54. I was not "man enough" to go to her funeral. I was totally distraught & I just could not do it, I know that is no excuse & I have been truly ashamed of myself ever since. I have often wondered if my life would have been any different if that tragic accident hadn't happened.

It wasn't long before I started going up to Wappenbury Hill a bit more for a while, well, actually till Doreen got married.

It was also about this time that Choggie's family moved to Stoneliegh into a new house. His lovely Mum had died much too early, that meant that not only had they lost a wife & a mum but we had lost her incredible knowledge of the natural world & it meant that Gwen (Gwenno) being the oldest girl became mum to her three younger siblings & what a darned good job she did of it too!

It was decided that the old thatched cottage that belonged to the Pub they had called home was to be demolished & Shorty (Doreen's dad) & Wilf were going to do the job! They started to strip the thatch & burn it, the fire was a bit too close to the cottage & whoosh the whole lot was ablaze. I don't know whether the Fire Brigade (from Leamington) were involved or not but it was left to burn, so all that was left was ashes, walls & a huge chimney which were soon removed & a new modern building put in its place, that there were many heated debates about.

Book Three
Just a country Kid
!1951 Full time Job

When I was looking to leave the College I had heard that Dick was leaving Mr Penelope's farm, so I went to see him about a job. When I got to the farm at Hunningham Hill it was obvious it was old fashioned, with no electricity & most jobs done with horses even though he had a Fordson tractor & instead of being a dairy farm this was very mixed, raising calves, sheep, cereals, mangolds & spuds on 178 acres (which happened to be my number at College). We had quite a chat with Arthur (Mr Penteloe) asking me if I was sure I was making the right decision leaving school. Anyway I got the job & was going to be paid nearly 3 quid a week including weekend feeding, with more during hay making & harvest.

There was something about Mr Penteloe (Arthur) & his wife Agnes (Agie) that I liked. Yes they were old fashioned & Arthur was known to be strict but I decided I would like to work for him. I left school on Maundy Thursday started work at 7 30 on Easter Saturday morning, watching how to feed calves & learning what to feed the other stock in the pens & pumping rain water from an underground tank for the stock (that job made your arms ache) we finished about 9 30 then started again at 4 o'clock till about 5 15. The same on Sunday & Bank Holiday Monday & then it was full time. Eventually when I had learnt "the ropes" a bit, I worked one Saturday afternoon & Sunday & Jack worked the next. Saturdays were worked till 12 30 as part of the normal week & everything that could be got ready for Sunday was done then

The farmhouse was just as it might have been a hundred years before, there was a yard in front of the back door, with a workshop along one side & a well in the middle, and this well was something special! It was over 120 feet to the water & to get the water up there was a contraption that as you turned the handle (for ages) a bucket came up full of water & another went down, when the bucket got to the top It caught on a rim the bottom opened & the water came out of the spout, (& to be fair it was beautiful clear sweet water), you then turned the handle the other way for the next bucket. It was really slow & if you turned the handle too fast the rising bucket would swing hit the side of the well & empty the water, which meant you had to wind it right to the top & start again (bloody nightmare), in front of two Pig Sties was the pump used for the stock. In the house, inside the back door was a big scullery with a boiler in the corner that always had lengths of wood sticking out with the ends alight, a big old table, a butter churn & a pantry with a marble shelf. Along the passage was the Breakfast room with a black range where the cooking was done, then onto the Dining room where they lived & there was always a roaring fire (Agie always had Corn beef legs through sitting too close to that fire when knitting) & then a Front room that was only used on High Days & Holidays & a front door into a garden that overlooked a pond, upstairs there were three bedrooms & a Bathroom! The water for the bath (hot & cold) had to be carried up in a bucket. The toilet was a building covered in ivy in the orchard about twenty yards from the house! Which was known as "the House of Lords" & was basically a board over a pit, just like we had at Hunningham School, though this one had ashes from the fires added, not sure if that was to kill the bugs. Through the Orchard were the Hen houses where the hens had free range & that was another of Agie's jobs feeding & collecting eggs, sometimes Arthur would spend a few hours in the hedge (without lighting his trusty pipe) with his Shot-gun ready because a Fox had raided the Hen house & killed quite a few. He usually put paid to the offender, because they nearly always seem to come back for the ones they couldn't carry first time.

Right next to the house were the farm buildings, starting with the Granary up 15 stone steps then another 5 to the second section, under the steps was the dog kennel where the sheep dogs lived. Next was the shed where the stock feed was mixed, through a gate into a yard first a loose box then a big old threshing barn that was now used for storing hay & as a stock pen, through another gate there were two more loose boxes & a shed where the corn was ground or rolled for the stock. In there was a brilliant old open crank engine (Ruston Hornsby) that drove the mill & roller, (horses only had rolled Oats not ground). It was quite an art starting this old girl! Which I had to learn, first making sure all the cups were full of oil (making sure you wiped round the first to make sure no dust got into them) Filling up, with water & petrol. Then turning the big flywheels backwards till you got to compression fit the handle on the main shaft & turn as fast as you could if you got it right it would start if you didn't it would kickback (that's when knowing about not putting your thumb over the handle came in handy). When the engine had been running for a while it would boil better than any kettle & would need topping up with water. Back in the yard were three more loose boxes & an open cattle shed along the back side there was a dung heap in the middle of the yard. By the open shed was a door that led to the second yard this had a loose box where the "house cow" was milked & then a shed where the small calves were kept & the nursing cows were tied up. Next door to that was the stable where the four horses were kept Boxer, Drummer, Beauty (a grey mare) & Jumbo. When used in pairs Drummer & Beauty worked together & Boxer & Jumbo. As Drummer had never been broken to shafts he was only used as a Fore horse for Beauty or alongside but only in chains. Above the stable was a hay loft that was filled through a small window this was an open yard with a roof on two sides & hay rack all the way round, the stock had free run in & out & it was used mostly in winter. There was a Rick-yard behind the big barn where the Corn-ricks were built, (the Hay ricks were built in the field the hay came from usually), & Agie kept her fire wood, By the Rick-yard alongside the drive was a covered shed for the Machinery, the Tractor & fuel tank. The tractor was only used for four jobs, Ploughing, Cambridge Rolling, Hay sweeping & pulling the Corn Binder, it had Steel wheels with strakes on the rear that made square holes in the ground & a rim on the front for grip, everything else was done with horses the way it had been done for 100s of years! The Tractor was fine in a field but when you had to cross the Fosse Way It nearly shook you to bits no matter how slow you went. Arthur always insisted that you greased all round every time the Tractor was used including turning the grease cap on the water pump a half a turn, & drained the water when you finished. He always said "Boy, grease is the cheapest spare part you can buy" something I carried with me all my working life. I had driven a Fordson at Robsons but I had only done some scuffling so I had a lot to learn Arthur was an excellent teacher though he hated Tractors, he never had a car & before he bought a little James Motor Bike used to either cycle or get a lift wherever he went, I think he only bought that because a friend of his from Leamington (Jack) used to sell them. It was a sight to behold Arthur on his James with his Trilby on & his pipe in his mouth going to Warwick market, he only ever used it to go to market.

Arthur introduced me to his other employee Jack who I actually knew because he lived in the cottage two doors from us that was Tied to Penteloe's farm, he was married with two young children & joined my Dad nearly every night at the Plough.

Jack was another horse-man through & through who loved to tell of using teams of six or eight horses hauling timber. He was just the sort of person to help me learn more about how to put on the different harness & handle horses either singly or in pairs, how to hitch them up to a pole, fixing the chains to a Swingletree (or Sweltree these were either strong wooden or U shape steel that were bow shaped in the centre was metal band fixed & a shackle that fixed to the implement at both ends were rings that the chains fixed to. The Swingletree was just wider than the horse & was ideally at least three feet from the ground so the horses didn't get their legs caught in them) & their Collars to the Pole-bar, joining their heads with a chain about two feet long, running the rope reins through the Collar rings. My first go at driving two abreast was using a mower cutting a big batch of thistles. I used Boxer & Jumbo because it was decided I needed a bit of practice before I used Drummer & Beauty, because Drummer had a habit of playing up, trying to rear up & generally being a nuisance, especially if you raised your voice to him (never knew why Arthur wouldn't get rid of him). Arthur always said it was because "he was cut late" (castrated or Gelded) which also perhaps explained his thick Stallion neck & how he danced when he was "on his Toes". I thought it was going to be easy sitting on the seat & just driving them, I soon learnt that every time you had a blockage on the mower blade you had to pull the mower back a yard or so as the horses in chains had no means of pushing it back remembering to knock it out of gear in case there was movement while clearing the knife which was driven by the wheels, & if the knife was getting a bit blunt & was making it harder to pull the mower the horses would keep stopping as they got used to stopping when there was a blockage & if you were facing downhill it was bloody hard sweaty work, that made you swear even if it didn't help much.

Hay making

My first year during hay making Jack did the mowing & I was shown how to sharpen the mower blades with a file, the knife was clamped to the top rail of the gate of the field you were mowing & you filed the sections just enough to sharpen them but not enough to wear them out, if a section became loose after hit a stone, you had a hammer, punch & dolly to replace it. The pair of horses were changed at dinner time, they never worked for a whole day on that sort of work. After the grass was cut for a day or so I was allowed to use one of the horses with the Dicky Turner that turned the grass over, it was a machine that had two circle of tines that turned driven by its wheels. The tines had to be set so they just missed the ground or they very easily broke & you didn't want bit of spring steel in the hay.

Once the hay was ready after Tedding (spreading out to dry) & then being put into rows. I had my first job on the Tractor, I was going to use the Hay-sweep, It was like a big comb fixed to the front axle of the Tractor with long wooden tines made of Ash, with a steel point, the idea was you drove along a row of hay & pushed the heap to the elevator so it could be taken up to Arthur & Ernie (if he was available) building the Hay-rick. To build a rick of loose Hay, that would stand up & not let in water was perhaps the most skilled job on a farm & a job I never did. The person (Jack) loading the elevator would either yell at you that he was waiting or you were bringing too much! I learnt that when you were going to the far side of the field & it took you a bit longer it stopped him yelling about waiting if you pushed some hay one way then went round & pushed some from the other side, it meant it took longer for him to load onto the elevator!. The thing you could not do with a sweep was turn sharp if you did you broke the wooden tines & then there was trouble (Arthur didn't believe you should ever break anything) but sweeping was by far the easiest job at Hay making time, at 3 o'clock Agie would bring out Tea. Which was always Home-made bread, butter & jam with a huge jug of tea, to sit in a field eating & drinking, for someone brought up on Margarine that home-made butter was superb & that was as good as it gets. After the sweeping was finished the horse rake would be brought out & the hand rakes getting every bit out of the corners so everything you had missed would be raked into lines & then swept up to the elevator it was amazing how much was found & if Arthur had got it right topped the rick up nicely (he usually had)

A metal rod with a barb on the end was regularly pushed into the rick them pulled out, the barb would pull some hay from the middle of the rick (this was done to be sure the hay wasn't getting hot, as it could if some wasn't really dry & if it got hot enough it would ignite) If a rick started to get warm you pulled loose hay from the leeward side to let the heat out & if that didn't work you pulled the loose from the windward side to get more cold air in, it was when a rick got warm that it was liable to need wooden props to stop it falling (Arthur's rick hardly ever needed a prop). When you came to take hay out of the rick you used a Hay Knife, it was quite an amazing tool to work with, it had a blade about feet three long, built like a Scythe blade but wider with a handle at right angle to the blade, the important thing was to keep it sharp just like a Scythe. You put your weight on the blade cutting into the hay then lifted it up moved it along a bit & did it again, the whole idea was you cut out two sides of a square the other side were the corner of the Rick, It took a bit of getting the hang of but eventually it became a bit easier to do. The hay could then be carried on a fork in flakes.

Livestock

I got used to the routine of feeding the stock but the one job I hated was milking the "house cow" she was a Jersey (because the milk is rich & good for making butter) she just did not like being milked & as soon as you sat down on the stool she would kick out & snort, putting your head in her groin gave you a bit of a warning as you felt the muscles tighten but you still didn't get the bucket out of the way & what milk you had got was lost. We tried the trick of a rope round her belly, even a rope over her back in a stall to keep her down but the damn thing still managed to kick & to be honest I was a bit scared of her (& she bloody knew it) many times on my weekend on I had to get Arthur to come & hold her tail up (Which makes it difficult for a cow to kick), just so I could milk the thing, I was very pleased when she went dry & was sold so we had a new one that was much more amenable.

Something I soon noticed was round the eyes & ears of some of the young stock was like crusty arears, when I asked what it was Arthur said "Oh that's just Ringworm young stock often get it". It wasn't long before I bloody got it too! I had these places come on my arms, my face well pretty well everywhere except in my hair, so it was a trip to Princethorpe to the doctor & yes I had got Ringworm & was given some purple stuff to put on it (Gel of Violets I think) so for about six months I looked a bit like a clown gone wrong or an accident in a paint store, with those purple patches that got bigger before they got better. I don't know if some people are more prone to

Ringworm than others but I didn't see Arthur or any of the others with it. When the purple stuff got rid of it or my body built up a resistance to it I never caught it again but the calves still had it. Learning how to get some calves to suckle was difficult at times. If calves were cheap at the market there were always some that you felt had never suckled a cow & no matter how patient the suckle cows were (There were usually four) by the time you had got the calf to suckle they were a bit fidgety, each cow would have three or four calves suckling sometimes more in shifts! Not all the calves were bought in, home raised heifers were put in calf usually by AI (Artificial Insemination) as Arthur didn't like having a Bull around as most of the fields had footpaths through. When they calved if they were good enough they were sold & the calf kept. If they were not good enough they became suckle cows. Suckle cows were either Inseminated again when they came into season or fattened & sold for meat. In the spring all the cattle would be brought into a yard & their backs were sprayed with a Jeyes Fluid mix to keep of the Warble Fly. Some young stock when they were let out to grass in the spring caught "Lung Worm" a little worm that lays in the grass is digested by the animal then gets into its lungs & makes it cough. The animal soon loses condition. The cure then was to Drench (pour liquid down their throat) them with a mixture of Chlorophorm. As we hadn't got a cattle crush, we had to catch & nose (put your finger & thumb up their nose & squeeze) them & hold tight till the Drench was down their throat. Believe me it was like a Rodeo without the ropes! It was not only hard work but the fumes from the Chlorophorm in the air when the animal coughed made you a bit unsteady on your feet. Nosing was used a lot for controlling cattle, but there is also a tool called a Bull-dog that does the same thing but is perhaps a bit more brutal. Why we never had a "Cattle Crush" was beyond me, as it would have made life a darn sight easier. Having a lot of young stock around & regularly calving Heifers there was always going to be losses & problems (sometimes perhaps because the animal was too young) which meant a visit from the Knacker Man to take the fallen animal away or if it was ill & not going to get better it was dispatched in the back of the truck. I remember one little heifer trying to calve prematurely & she damaged her back, we put her in a sling so her feet were just touching the floor & I finally after a lot of pulling got a beautiful part Jersey calf out, it was so premature it's hooves hadn.t formed & it was very weak. It's Mum had no milk to give it a start in life So I spent days & nights squirting milk down it's throat until it started to suckle (provided I held it up) after about five weeks I started to just about stand on its own & I was chuffed to bits because Arthur said it wasn't going to survive (that's why I struggled) alas about a week later he was right & it died. We also had a Cow that had been used for suckling calves, but when she calved she went totally mad & started to bunt her calf in the air, it was decided we had to get the calf out, so I sneaked into the loose box but as I got near the calf the cow saw me & I jumped from the manger into the hay rack just out of her reach & stayed there till Chris let the cow out to go racing round the yard (why the Hell we didn't do that in the first place is anyone's guess) but when I finally ventured out of the loose box with a calf that was a bit battered but OK Chris was outside the yard after vaulting the gate after the cow chased him. I think I only got out so easily because Chris had got that mad cows attention alas she also finished in the knacker Man's truck.

If Arthur bought any stock from Warwick market it was always delivered by a stock dealer friend of his who came from around Warwick way I think, Arthur would also buy stock off him as well, I sometimes used to think only because it was cheap & no one else wanted it. I remember once he bought two Heifers & when the back of the cattle Truck was opened one of them bolted out ran across the field like a race horse jumped the hedge & that was the last we saw of it. There were lots of phone calls to other farmers but it was never found which was quite good really as I certainly didn't fancy trying to handle something like that. If calves were cheap we would have loads & if they were small he always said "they have got all the world to grow in"

Sheep

Arthur also had about Sixty Sheep including two Rams, a mixed bunch of breeds, depending what was cheap when he was buying. The sheep & the outdoor stock around the farm were mostly looked after by Arthur & you could always tell where he was because of the puffs of smoke from his pipe (I think he only took it out of his mouth to either refill it or eat, there was always the joke that he slept with it in his mouth,) but to be honest he never lit his pipe in the rick-yard or on a hay rick, he smoked a mixture of Twist & Player's flake.

When I started work at Arthur's Lambing was just about finished so one of the first jobs I ever did with Sheep was cutting Lamb's tails & castrating the males. The Sheep & Lambs were brought in from the field behind the house & put in the sheep-pen at the end of the Rick-yard. A fire was lit & three tools were put in to heat up, They were like chisels with a blade about two inches wide, a shaft about ten inches long with a wooden handle, there was also a tin of Stockholm Tar & a sharp knife, pair of, well they looked like scissors with the ends bent over & flattened. When the tools were glowing in the fire I was shown how to catch a lamb & hold it with two legs in each hand & sit it on a wooden block holding its legs apart, It's tail was then held by Arthur who had one of the chisel things in his hand he then pushed onto the tail & cut it off nice & short, the hot iron not only cutting off the tail but also sealing the wound. If it was a male Lamb while it was sitting on the block the bottom of the scrotum was cut off with the sharp pen knife & the two balls pulled out with the Scissor tool & dab of Stockholm Tar was put on the cut to stop infection & Flies. The Lamb sent back to its Mum walking a bit groggy for a few minutes but I could hardly believe how quickly they got over such a thing. The tails were all put in a bag at the end because Choggie's family used to make a meal out of them! At the end of the day I was shown how Castration used to be done, you held the Lamb the same with two hands but on you shoulder The Scrotum was then cut & the balls pulled out by the other person using their teeth, (Yuk I know they were known as Sweat-breads but you needed a strong stomach for that). A couple of years later the system of using rubber bands for doing the same jobs was used. The rubber bands were put on the tail & scrotum (making sure the balls had dropped & keeping fingers away from the band) using a stretcher then releasing the ring it cut off the blood supply & the tail, etc., fell off a couple of weeks later. This was a much less barbaric way with no chance of infection & the Lamb's seemed to hardly notice. But there were no more Lamb's tails for tea.

The next job was to clean up the wool on the sheep's backside, the wool that had sh-t on it was cut off (Dagging) this was done with the old style hand shears, that really made your hand ache when you first had a go because you had to keep pressure on the spring to keep the blades together. The sheep was turned over & sat down because in that position you have control. Its feet were checked & trimmed if needed & any sign of Foot-rot was treated with Stockholm Tar. Dagging was done so that the fleece was clean when it was shorn & also to keep away the flies that laid eggs in it that turned into maggots that actually ate the sheep's flesh(if you found maggots you rubbed off what you could & then put neat Jeyes Fluid onto the area the maggots then dropped off). The Dags were usually put in a bag & gardeners had them to put in a drum with water to make brilliant fertilizer.

In June after a couple of warm days if you could fit it in with haymaking came Shearing, Arthur had a Lister petrol engine on a trolley with two belt driven Shearing heads with flexible drives to hand-pieces or shears. The Combs & Cutters from the shears were sent away to be sharpened every year as it was vital for shearing they were kept sharp. I found out you needed two warm days before shearing & you penned the sheep up tight so they would get hot & "wool would come up" well not really the wool but the grease in it, if the grease hadn't risen it was nearly impossible to shear a sheep with a mechanical shear. Anyway my first year was spent catching the sheep & bringing them out of the pen, making sure no others could escape. I was then showed how to "Tie a Fleece" by stretching it out on a tarpaulin the folding the sides in, rolling it up nearly to the end making sure you put any odd bits in, when you get nearly to the end you knelt on the fleece then pulled & twisted the remaining wool into a rope, making sure you didn't pull it off the fleece, you the wrapped the rope round the rolled fleece & tucked in the end. It was said that if you did it properly you could play football with it. It was hot sweaty work & Arthur & Jack who were shearing had a supply of bottles of beer to keep them going & when I was offered one I didn't say no. I did alright in the morning but in the afternoon I mucked up a couple of fleeces, perhaps I got a bit cocky (I was told a well rolled fleeces was worth more than bad ones) & Arthur decided if I couldn't do better than that I ought to go & dig Docks. Docks in cornfields were a menace (the only thing Docks are good for is rubbing the leaves on nettle stings) before sprays were used, you had a Fork that had one tine that had a V on the end, you put the V under the dock root & dug it out (in theory) quite often you missed the root & had to have another go. I was told "you must get every bit or it will grow again", the damn things came back every year anyway! Faced with a big patch of the things on your own, was a most soul destroying job & even worse than spreading Ant-hills.

I made sure I tied the fleeces properly the next time, Digging Docks, pulling Charlock & Wild Oats were bad enough jobs when there were three of you but on your own was bloody awful, especially in the rain when the soil sticks to your boots.

The next year I was given the second Hand-piece, shown how to shear & told to get on with it & I did! OK it was sweaty work that made your arms & back ache but it got you fit & it was better than digging Docks & of course there was always a bottle of beer handy.

I had to wait until the next spring before I learnt about Lambing, learning how to help a ewe lamb, how to put your hand inside her & turn a lamb that was coming backwards (that took some learning) & how to make sure a lamb could breathe properly after it was born. I also learnt (slowly) the art of getting a ewe that had lost a lamb, to adopt another lamb, with the last resort of skinning her dead lamb & fitting the skin to the adoptee that usually worked. If it didn't that lamb would be fed on a bottle & was known as a "Cade" there were always a few of those following Agie around as she fed those. Sometimes becoming a nuisance as after a while they thought every human was Mum! A big proportion of lambs are born at night & if the weather was not too bad the sheep were left in the field behind the farm buildings, it's a big hill with a flat piece at the top by those buildings, and there was also a row of big trees that partly divided the flat piece from the hill. I was also where the horses grazed when not in the stable. During Lambing Arthur would spend most of the night out with the sheep, on my second year it was decided that him & I would do alternate nights. There was nothing more terrifying for a sixteen year old, than sitting under a tree In the middle of the night & hearing a sheep cough or horses snuffle as they grazed you would imagine all sorts of things.

Occasionally I would go to work on the old Sloper & Arthur would say "hide the damn thing at the back of the shed in case Johnny (the local Bobby) sees it" Arthur was a Special Police Sargent with the same powers as a PC but thankfully turned a blind eye to my stupidity. He did have to do duties but only on foot or pushbike. I think Johnny only used to call in for a cup of tea & a piece of Agie's cake, whenever he was going round his beat showing his face.

A job that was a long walk was Sheep dipping time, the Sheep Dip (a long narrow brick built pool with a flat piece at one end & steps at the other) was at Wappenbury on Sir William Lyon's farm (he was MD at Jaguar Cars after first becoming famous for designing a Sidecar & then lived in the beautiful Wappenbury Hall) & was used by all local farmers. So the sheep were driven along the Fosse Way to Eathorpe & then over the river bridge & up the hill to Wappenbury, being on the road was good for their feet as it wore away the excess on their Clays. Arriving at the Dip The Local PC would be there (Johnny) to check the right amount of Chemical was added to the water, then each sheep was caught & slid bum first into the mixture, the animal had to be totally immersed twice before it could climb out up the steps & stand in an area where the liquid would drain off & run back into the dip. Sheep had to be dipped to prevent Sheep Scab (which it highly contagious) & Ticks. The sheep-dogs were also put in to get rid of ticks & fleas & just for a bath. The PC was there to watch every sheep was dipped & had to fill in the appropriate forms. Driving the sheep to & from the dip was usually timed to miss any local delivery Lorries.

Harvest Time

When the corn was getting nearly ripe it was time to pull Wild Oats & Charlock, these weeds showed above the corn, so there was no excuse to miss any, you pulled them up & carried them under your arm till you got to the hedge putting them in heaps to be collected & burned, not the best job in the world but weed-killer sprays were not around then (well certainly not at Arthur's). We grew Wheat, Barley, Oats & Beans. Winter Barley was always first to ripen.

The Binder was checked & the canvases (that carried the corn from the Cutter to the Knotter) were fitted, the Knife was sharpened & everything was lubricated. Arthur & Jack (he knew what he was talking about) then spent quite a while telling me how the knotter worked & how to find the fault from the prior knot if there was a problem (this was to stand me in good stead years on).

Before the Tractor & Binder entered the field, the width of them both was cut round the field with a Scythe so that no standing corn was damaged & the corn was then tied into Sheaves by hand (the corn was collect onto your knees & then a band as made of straw tied around & the ends tucked in (if you did it right, after a bit of practice it would hold like string). My job that year was tying Sheaves as I don't think they fancied being in the same field as me swinging a Scythe!

We then came to the Tractor bit, after a couple of swings I got it going, then it was getting the Binder through the gate-way without hitting the posts, even though it was being pulled side-ways on two removable wheels & the drawbar fixed to the "Bed", it was a bit tight & I so wanted to get through OK & I did! The drawbar was then fitted to the front & the two wheels removed, so that the driving wheel & the Bed wheel were on the ground. Everything was driven by an open link chain from the driving wheel. I was told I needed to be in second gear & to make sure I watched the Binder to make sure I took a full cut but didn't miss any & most important of all if there was a yell, stop!. Off we went me on the Tractor & Arthur on the Binder, Jack was joining the two local women who had come to put the sheaves into Stooks. I soon got the hang of it & didn't get into trouble all day, in fact at the end of the day I was told "Boy you did that OK" (Arthur always called me Boy) When we were near to finishing Arthur always had his Shot-gun with him & Wilf from Hunningham who also went Rabbiting, would have his gun & as the Rabbits or Foxes ran out of the corn they were shot, the people doing the Stooking always stood well back for a few minutes. Arthur even sitting on the Binder seat rarely missed. Rabbits at that time were really a menace (even though they were a major part of the diet of some people). They would clear whole areas of crops particularly near a large Burrow. Most farmers encouraged people to go ferreting. When the field was finished we would help those Stooking, again I had to be shown how to do it properly, even though I thought I knew how to do it. As you carried the sheaves under your arms to put them together, the inside of your arms got very sore especially if there were Thistles in the Straw, but the women who went from farm to farm somehow managed very well. I soon learnt that even though I didn't normally wear a shirt that time of the year I always had an old long sleeved one to put on for that job. Sometimes at weekends Dad & Jack (Nina's husband who would come on holiday at that time) would also come & help.

When the corn stood upright it was quite easy on the Binder, just adjusting the sails occasionally to keep the corn off the knife & checking that the sheaves were tied OK. But if the corn had been battered down by the weather or Badgers rolling in it, it was a very different job, to get the corn over the knife you had to walk behind the cutter be with a hooked stick & keep pulling the corn & watching you don't get wacked by the sails, obviously the Tractor was going very slow in first gear but it was a horrendous job, not just the pulling but you had to wear leather Gaiters to protect your shins from bumping against the cutter bed, I was always very pleased to be on the Tractor even though I learnt some fancy swearwords. Oats were very difficult to harvest if they had been battered & were the most at risk, because of the soft straw & large heads. They were a crop like Beans you either did very well out of them or lost a lot of money. Beans were a nightmare you had to wait until the crop was nearly black, then you cut round the field with a Scythe & whoever was picking up & tying had to carry string to tie the sheaves. Beans never went over the knife well so Arthur was working the sails up & down all the while. One year I remember the beans were so badly battered that they had to be left where they lay & the sheep turned on the to eat them.

The Stooks were left in the field "to hear the church bells twice" to dry the straw & for the weeds to die off, well, that's how it is supposed to work. If it rained it took longer & sometimes the Stooks would have to be taken apart & rebuilt, if the rain had been really bad the grains would start to grow & you would have to pull the Sheaves apart, if they had started to grow even when the corn was dry it couldn't be sold & could only be kept for stock feed.

During WW11 the church bells were not allowed to be rung each Sunday because they were only to be used as an alarm in case of invasion, this was relaxed in 1942 when the risk of invasion got a lot less & to hear the bells from the Priory at Princethorpe as you walk up the hill was brilliant.

Once everything was dry the sheaves had to be carted to the rick-yard, an area the size of a rick was covered in hedge cuttings saved from Hedge brushing, about two feet thick, to keep the corn off the ground. Waggons had been put in the pond overnight to make sure the tyres were tight on the Felloes (a waggon or cart wheel was made of Elm Hub, Oak Spokes & Ash or Elm Felloes with an iron Rim). Horses harnessed up & the Gang assembled, Three in the field two pitching the Sheaves & one loading the waggon (a very skilled Job as each Sheaf locked the next, if they didn't the load would fall off, that didn't happen very often but if it did you were in for a Rollicking) One driving horses(Jack) & three in the Rick-yard, Arthur on the Rick usually with Ernie(from Weston under Wetherley (who could never come on a Sunday as he played the organ in church), you had to pass the sheaves with a fork corn end first, & Wilf on the load feeding the elevator. As the waggon was loaded in the field one of the pitchers moving the horse on to each Stook, (though after a couple of days the horses learnt when to move on themselves), when loaded it would be tied down with a rope & the Fore horse (that used chains the same as when working two abreast except there was a pole fitted about a foot behind the horse's tail to keep the chains apart) would be hooked on to the two loops on the waggon shafts at the gate, then setting off, no matter which field you came from it was uphill to the Rick-yard & the last bit of the Fosse Way before you turned onto the Farm drive was quite steep, so the horses were pushed on to a trot to make sure they made it(never knew them to fail), that meant that the Waggoner (who was driving the Fore horse from the side of the horse in the shafts that knew how to follow its leader) was running to keep up. The horses soon remembered each time when to speed up. If the field was one of the furthest from the Rick-yard three waggons would be used one loading one travelling & one being unloaded which meant Drummer was kept busy being fore horse. On the way back empty it was a bit more leisurely, but coming down hill because Drummer was usually dancing about, Beauty would be sitting in the Breaching trying to keep the wagon back, Boxer & Jumbo were a lot easier, though Boxer would rather trot than walk & Jumbo just grunted & thought of food he was just lazy, but a hell of a character, well actually they were all characters & even though there were times you felt like shooting them, they also made you laugh (& sweat). My first year I was in the field pitching Sheaves onto the waggon, after being shown how to do it without breaking the Pitch Fork Handle. Before the end of harvest I had driven the horses up to the Rick-yard & had a go at loading a waggon & the load stayed on!

In the Rick-yard Arthur would start the Rick by making a Stook in the middle of the Hedge Brushings, & then work outwards keeping the ears of corn upmost. The Sheaves were put in layers with each sheaf locking the next, making sure you kept the corners square & that the centre was at least two feet higher than the sides, this was to allow for the Rick settling (the centre being heaviest settles the most) if the centre finished lower than the outside the rainwater would run in but if you built the roof right as well you could just about get away without thatching, but not usually a good idea.

If there was a chance that the straw was a bit damp, when building the Rick, a sack would be filled with straw, then put in middle & built round pulling the sack upwards every other layer. You would then finish up with a chimney to release the heat, particularly Oats as the straw is soft & can hold moisture. I remember one year having to take an Oat Rick down because it was so hot it was in danger of Instantaneous Combustion, it was not rebuilt. Jim Berry's Threshing Drum was ordered, the gang assembled & the whole lot threshed, the straw that would normally been used as fodder was only good enough for bedding & the grain was so badly cooked that when Rolled had to be mixed with other feed to get the stock to eat it (even Jumbo turned his nose up a bit & he would eat anything) If a Rick was built right it rarely needed props to hold it up unless it did get a bit warm & then it would move. When you were on a Rick & getting near the top the whole thing used to be almost like standing on jelly & a bit scary until it settled.

During harvest in my second year Jack had moved on to pastures new & we had a fella from Coventry called Alan start work, he was a really nice fella but I don't think he knew as much as me but the cottage that went with the job meant somewhere for his wife & two young kids. We very soon became quite good friends & I often went to his house for a chat in the evenings.

Alan came up with an idea soon after arriving that as others made money catching Rabbits, we ought to have a go at earning a few bob. So I bought two Ferrets, he built a hutch & they were kept in his Pig Sty, I bought a few Purse Nets, we got some line & small collars. It was decided that as I had bought the Ferrets Alan would feed & look after them. I bought a Jill (female) that looked like a Polecat & Hob (male) that was a large Albino from Hunningham. So on Sunday mornings we started Rabbiting, I knew enough about it to say it was a waste of time putting the Ferret in the Big Burrows, as the rabbits could give them the run-around & you could never net all the holes, so we worked the hedgerows. A collar with a cord attached was put on the Ferret & the Ferret was put in the Rabbit hole, after checking for other holes that might be connected & putting Purse Nets over them, if the Ferret came straight out there was no-one at home but if there was hopefully the Rabbit bolted out of a hole you had netted & you had it, but sometimes the Rabbit stood its ground & the Ferret would grab it (when a Ferret bites it doesn't let go as we were to learn, the Jill had to be handled carefully or she would have you, & the only way to get her off was squeeze her neck till her eyes nearly popped out then she would let go). Then if you put your ear to the ground you could hear the battle going on. You could tell how far the Ferret had gone by the amount of cord used & if you listened carefully you could find the spot to start digging, you dug as quickly as possible so the Ferret didn't start eating the Rabbit, because one the Rabbit would be worthless & two you would have one Hell of a job getting the Ferret back. We did catch quite a few Rabbits but soon found that one of the Ferrets the Hob was useless, it wouldn't work on a line & often would just stay in a hole for the Hell of it. Any way one Sunday we took both Ferrets out put one in on the line & the other loose, after spending a couple of hours waiting for the loose one to reappear we left it! To be told some weeks later someone had seen a Ferret not far from where we lost it. We didn't go looking for it I bought another Jill instead. Dad started coming along & he was good with a spade, one Sunday we were working at the side of a pond, we had netted the holes & put the Ferret in the hole, immediately a Rabbit bolted out of a hole we had missed & knocked dad off balance sending him straight into the water (what a photo that would have been), we also had an experience at another pond, we put the Ferret in a hole there was a Hell of a commotion underground, the Ferret came out literally shaking followed by a very angry Moorhen! We never made money from Rabbiting but we had some fun & we were all upset when the Ferrets died & we never really knew why.

Because Alan hadn't any experience with them I had more driving of horses & loading waggons. One late evening in August, we had two more loads to do & a storm started to blow up one waggon was half loaded & the other with Beauty in the Shafts waiting, well she knew something was going to happen! She took off home followed by Jumbo me falling off the half load, & all three of us in the field started running after them, getting wet through because the heavens opened. The two horses & waggons didn't stop till they got to the rick-yard! They had gone through two gate ways & across the Fosse Way, that day we were not using fore-horses as there was no big hill. By the time we had finished sheeting up & putting the Horses to bed we were soaked to the skin, then there was a huge bang & a building by where Eric used to live had been struck by Lightning & was on fire, being up on a hill it was a spectacular sight, at first we were worried it might have been a house. The date was 10 August 1952 the same night that Lynmouth in Devon was nearly wiped out with floods. Arthur always said he had never known the horses to go home alone before.

Occasionally a Waggon or Cart would have to go to the Wheelwrights for repairs to wheels, the workshop was on a hill (Bascote I think) outside Long Ichington, which meant driving the horse to Long Itchington (riding on the waggon was allowed because it was empty) but you had to go through a Ford & as the horses were not used to being driven through water, you had to walk them through, getting drenched from the splashes & also on the way back.

I had a very scary experience with Boxer after I had been doing some fencing, in a field along the gated road, on the way back to the farm coming down the hill all of a sudden Boxer snorted & took off with me hanging onto his Bridle & the end of the shaft, my feet rarely touching the ground. I knew there was a gate soon & I expected him to stop, he didn't, he tried to jump the gate with the waggon behind instead & me hanging on "for grim Death" after going through the gate (which was smashed) I let go & as I landed the Waggon wheel touched the shoulder of my coat! I damaged my knee but got up & saw Boxer in the distance, standing waiting at the next gate. I hobbled along the road & when I got to him he was trembling but just had a small scratch on his chest. I got him to back up a bit so I could open the gate & noticed that the Breaching was a bit loose, so I was sure he caught his back leg on the Waggon as we came down the hill & that's what spooked him. When I got back to the farm & told Arthur, I got one Hell of a Bollocking for breaking the gate & he didn't even ask how I was! But fair dues he did the next morning when he had cooled down a bit. That knee alas has always had a problem since then but it could have been a lot worse. One night the horses broke out of the field & got on the Fosse way George unfortunately ran into Boxer cutting the horse's chest. After picking himself up, George knocked on Arthur's door got him out of bed & they got the horses back home. Luckily George was only a bit shaken up, his bike had a bent mudguard, twisted number plate & a few scratches on the exhaust but Boxer needed the cut dressing for a few weeks & got a bit uppity dancing about & being a damn nuisance when he saw a motorbike.

Twice during the summer Arthur's friend Jack's Daughter & a friend came to stay for a week's holiday, they were two very attractive girls. They were about sixteen & a bit flirty! They were also Teasers as their bedroom window overlooked the Cattle-yard they kept appearing in the window with nothing or next to nothing on. The other guy working there at the time was married with a small child & pretended he hadn't seen anything but my hormones were doing somersaults. Of course I became very interested even though I was a bit worried about what Arthur would say. Though he did surprise me one day as we were walking along the drive I said "I think that Heifer is bulling (in season") He replied nodding to the two girls "I'm damn sure they are". But after a bit of encouragement from Jack's daughter I had two weeks of snogging & groping. And a little bit with the other one, it's amazing what you could do between the mudguards on a Ford Standard. It was only for two weeks but it was darned well, even though I was more than a bit afraid of Arthur catching us.

Hedge cutting & laying

One of the winter jobs was when a hedge got too tall it usually got lots of holes in it & instead of filling the with a fence, you cut & laid them. The idea being that new shoots would grow from the cut stumps. It was done in the winter as the hedges were without leaves & the sap was not up. Arthur was a master of the art of cutting & laying a hedge, yes it is an art. First you learn how to sharpen an Axe, a Billhook & a Slashing-hook, you would have one of each & it was up to you to look after it. If you were right handed you had a very thick leather Left hand Hedging Glove & if you were kaki handed vice versa, that you used to hold the pieces you were cutting usually while standing on a slippery ditch bank trying hard not to get wet. I spent a lot of time with Arthur cutting out dead wood (that was to be collected & used for firewood) & Brambles, as he showed me which pieces to lay, how to trim them ready & how to cut them as near as possible to ground level & at the right angle with just enough wood left so they could be laid down without breaking off. He also taught me which varieties you couldn't lay because they would break off, Maple& Elder. But if there was nothing else you could leave Ash but Hawthorn or Blackthorn were used where possible to make a good Hedge, with Hazel because it is straight & supple used for Stakes & the Bands that held the Laid pieces in place. The Stakes in Warwickshire were cut level at the top with a saw (it was said that it was done that way so that if a rider at the Hunt jumped the hedge the stakes wouldn't scratch the horse's belly) but in some Counties were cut at an angle with a Billhook. I am not going to pretend I didn't have pieces break off particularly when I first started but I can say I DID learn the art of Cutting & Laying a Hedge maybe not to Competition standard but my Hedges, & I did quite a few, grew & were Stock-proof. I say stock proof but there were always the odd sheep that would wriggle though anything! That sheep had to be fitted with a collar made out of three Hazel stakes about three feet long tied round the sheep's neck in a triangle, which meant it couldn't push through a hedge, I know it may sound brutal but it worked.

Ploughing

Once the harvest was done it was time to get ready for the next part of the year. To plough the land ready to plant new crops. I had never done any ploughing, though I had seen it done all my life. There was a lot for Arthur to teach me, how to set the width of the front furrow (there were two on this Oliver plough) how to set the skims & discs & how to set the depth you were going to plough. He then taught me how to "Spilt a Ridge" (start) & how to finish a Furrow. He taught me how to mark out the headland & how to drive straight when you were "Splitting the Ridge". He also taught me how to turn into the Furrow so it was kept straight. I know I didn't always get it right at first, but I am not boasting when I say "I became damn good at it". One of the things I had to learn about the plough was to check the "drop legs" were working, particularly the little rear one as sometimes it could be wedged with a stone. The "Drop Legs" meant that when the plough dropped ready to go into the ground, instead of the plough dropping on the shares the legs took the weight & slowly let the plough down as you moved forward, meaning you didn't snap the share in half especially if the ground was hard. Arthur always said" it's bad enough wearing Shares out but it's bloody stupid to break them" I soon learnt that as you were plough round the Headland & getting near the Hedge if there were trees in the Hedge (particularly Ash as the roots a very near the surface) you drove on tick over so if you hit a root it stalled the tractor instead of breaking something. You then sometimes had a hell of a job to start the thing again (Petrol/TVO engines were noted for being difficult to start when hot)

One thing I learnt from Chris (David's dad) was that when you were ploughing with a Fordson Standard once the tractor was in the furrow & the front wheel was touching the furrow wall you could get off & walk behind or adjust the plough & the old girl would keep going in a straight line, ready for you to hop on board again. No elf & safety then but I never heard of a tractor leaving the driver behind.

Arthur was a Horseman so he believed that though Horses needed some rest, Tractors didn't, so when I was ploughing he would take over at lunch time for an hour. Many times on returning from lunch, the front wheels of the Tractor would be in the ditch, with Arthur standing by Swearing at it because instead of standing on the clutch to stop he'd yelled "WHOA". After a bit of toing & froing I got it out, sometimes losing the hour he saved! The most important thing I learnt about ploughing was when you had finished you covered the Mouldboards & Skims with a layer of grease so they didn't rust, if they did you had the worst job ever, making the soil slide along them next time you used them. It was while ploughing in 1953 I think, I saw the first Rabbit with Myxomatosis, with its swollen head & closed eyes it was awful! In fact the first time Arthur saw one he cried. The decease had obviously been in the big Burrow on Rabbit Bury Hill for a while as there soon appeared more & more. We always picked them (they didn't run away because they couldn't see you & were slowly starving to death) & with a Knock from the side of your hand behind the ears they were dead. If I was ploughing I put them in the furrow & buried them, making sure it was between first & second furrow so you didn't run over them on the next run. I know they were a menace but Myxomatosis was the most awful thing ever & it was suggested it was introduced intentionally from Australia to control them. This obviously put an end to ferreting etc. as no-one wanted to eat rabbit now. To see those animals suffering was much worse than seeing a Fox with Mange & again they were a menace but it was bad to see them suffering, but at least they could run away

Mechanical bits

It was at this time I learned a very serious lesson. In the days of Petrol/ Paraffin engines spark plugs regularly needed cleaning as they "whiskered". Anyway I decided to remove the plugs because the Tractor wasn't starting well. In those day spark plug leads didn't have an insulated cover on the end, there was just a metal strip with a hole in, and so to remove the lead you had to unscrew the little cap. The Spark Plugs could be stripped down into three bits for cleaning. It was then I did the Cardinal Sin of removing a plug & then unscrewing the top off another. That may not seem important till you see that plug top disappear in the hole where a plug should be! I didn't know whether to pretend it hadn't happened but knew that would ruin the engine. So I had to go & tell Arthur, after one Hell of a B-llocking of which I seemed to have more than my share, he rang Glovers (the Agents) & a mechanic was dispatched who had a thick piece of wire put a blob of grease on the end & in no time had the offending screw cap in his hand, I never ever took a cap of a plug again when one plug was out! The only other time I did anything really stupid was some time after that episode I started the Fordson & they was an awful Knocking sound, I was sure the Big-ends had gone (I had heard that expression) & Arthur had never heard it before, so another phone call to Glovers. When the Mechanic arrived he found the fan belt had become slightly loose & had half turned on the top pulley so the fan blade was hitting it! Halleluiah no Big-ends had gone & it was then I learnt how to remove shims out of the fan pulley to tighten the belt, there was no Dynamo or Alternator to adjust the belt with. The only other time Glovers were involved was when Arthur decided the Tractor needed to be reconditioned, after they had finished the engine was so tight you couldn't swing it, so another tractor was borrowed & a belt was fitted between the belt pulleys, after throwing off the belt a few times the engine began to turn & then started. It was left running for the rest of the day & was OK next time. But you needed a bit of muscle. Tractors in those days didn't have electrics so no lights & the spark was created by a Magneto fitted with an impulse device to hold the spark until the piston was way over "Top Dead Centre" that way the engine was less liable to "Kick back" & also to spin the Magneto faster to make a better spark, when you were using the Armstrong Starter (starting handle). Being a "Wet Clutch" the pedal had to be latched down before starting the engine or it could take ages to engage a gear. The Clutch Pedal was also the only brake on the Fordson, so by latching it down the parking brake was also on, though with a worm & gear rear axle I don't think it would have ever ran away. A regular job in the summer was washing the bits of straw & hay out of the outside of the tractor radiator, this was done because the tractor began boiling easily. The tractor was driven so the front wheels were in the pond & a WW2 Stirrup pump was used to wash the offending stuff out as there was no tap to put a hose on, most houses had a Stirrup pump left over from WW2 then.

Thatching

When the Ricks had settled it was time to thatch them. During my first year I was taught how to "straighten straw" the string on a Truss of wheat straw that had been dampened with water was cut & the straw was brought onto your knees, (which meant your knees got very wet), & raked side-ways with either your fingers or a wooden rake with nails in. Wheat straw is used because it is straighter & harder than Oat or Barley straw so it doesn't absorb water so easily. When you had straightened an arm full (a tile) it was laid flat on a piece of string the next Tile would be placed at a slight angle to keep each one apart when you had ten or twelve Tiles, you tied them up with the string into a Bundle. A Bundle was just about as much as you could carry up a ladder on the Rick. Thatching a Rick is different to thatching a house Which is an Art, as the thatch is only temporary so nowhere near as thick, & each row of Tiles are held down with Binder twine & pegs made from Hazel wood. After a couple of years Straightening Straw I was allowed to have a go at thatching & I was quite pleased it not only looked OK but the winter gales didn't blow it all off & for quite a few years I must admit I stood back & admired my work after finishing a Rick even though climbing up & down & standing on the rungs of a ladder all day made your feet ache..

Threshing

Perhaps one of the biggest occasions on a farm was the arrival of the Threshing Drum. Jim Berry (from Offchurch) would arrive with his Case Tractor pulling his drum & a Trusser. The Threshing drum looked like a big box with lots of pulleys & belts on wheels. They were (& still are) quite incredible bits of kit, with the corn being threshed with a drum & concave, the straw being "walked" out of the back & the grain separated just like it is now with the new "all singing all dancing posh Combine Harvesters (which I later drove & got to know well.) The big difference being you are in an Air-conditioned cab so no dust & no 18 stone sacks to carry! They also cut the crop & the weed seeds are put back on the ground. The drives are either V belt (multi or single) or Hydraulic motors, while on the Threshing Drum everything was driven by flat belts made of canvas that on a damp day would be tight but on a hot dry day would stretch & start to slip, then Jim would get his old battered tin of Black Treacle out dip a stick in it then put a little on the offending belt & Hey Presto it did the job (Arthur sometimes used a bit of Stockholm Tar on the belt that drove the Corn-mill & it worked the same) The Drum used to sound like a weird Orchestra with hum of the drum & fan & the sound of the Crocodile Clips on the belts as the went over the pulleys at different speeds. The main belt from the tractor or earlier Traction Engine drove the Machine from the end that the grain came out & if the person "feeding" the drum put too much through the big long belt (8 inches wide) would start jumping about & the person "on the bags" had to watch closely in case it came the pulleys flew their way, no "Health & Safety" then. Jim was certainly a master at that job & if the straw was needed for thatching he knew how to protect it from damage.

Once he knew which rick he was Threshing he would drive up to it perhaps having to do a bit of shunting to get it right Then Level it up (the Drum had to be level so that the straw & corn past over the walkers, shakers & sieves evenly, he would then set the tractor so the Flat drive belt was in line & stayed on the Pulleys. To see Jim working was truly seeing a Master of his Craft. The Side Boards were then raised to make the top platform & the Trusser was connected at the rear of the Drum. Arthurs Elevator was open up & set behind the Trusser pointing towards where the Straw Rick was to be built. It was time for a cup of tea by then curtesy of Agie. The corn sacks would be got out, the ones we had darned or patched on very wet days or the Hudson or Railway bags if the Wheat was to be sold. The Scales & the Sack barrow just about completed the kit except a few Pitch Forks of course. All we needed now was the labour! Jim always brought a lady from Offchurch who was on the Drum with him, she cut the strings at the knots, saved them & laid the sheave down correctly so Jim could feed it in the Drum. Two men were needed on the cornrick, Whoever else was working for Arthur (there were a lot of men came to work for Arthur, I think mainly because a house went with the job, but many after a while found living with no running water etc. difficult & there were always other jobs then) & a patient from the Mental Hospital at Weston under Weatherly. At that time Patients (those who were able) could be hired to work on local farms & for Threshing Arthur always had Four (usually the same four), three being very good but one making up the number. One of the Patients would put the Straw Trusses onto the Elevator for Ernie & another Patient to build the Straw Rick. The fourth looked after the Chaff & Chavings just tidying up. I had the job of bagging the Grain, sewing up the bags with the string saved from the Sheaves & carrying them to either a Waggon or up the granary steps. If the Corn (Barley or Oats) was going to be used for feed it was put in sacks that we had repaired & weighed about One & a half hundred weight but if it was Wheat & was to be sold it was put in Railway Bags or Hudson bags & were filled to Two & a Quarter Hundredweight (18stone!) & they had to be weighed exactly. You had to be pretty sharp to weigh them out, stitch them up, put them on the sack lift, get them on your back, walk to the Granary steps, then up steps & be back at the drum for the next one. I must say the first year I did that job I was Sixteen & Two & a Quarter Hundredweight made my legs tremble but I got stronger! When you were Threshing Oats the grain came out of the Drum quicker but was lighter even then it made you sweat even in the winter & it was no good yelling to Jim to slow down as he had his own speed! G-d help you if you had a bag overflow. Arthur quite often was missing while we had Patients working as for some reason he couldn't work with them, even though he employed them, so it soon became my job to sort what people did. Well it always seemed to work, at 10 o'clock Agie would bring out a big jug of tea & we would stop for ten minutes (she would also bring out four fags for the Patients, two smoked & the others saved theirs to sell at the hospital. You just had to make sure no-one smoked in the Rick-yard, Arthur always said by giving the fags at break time you knew where they were smoking) At lunch time Agie always brought out a big tray of Sandwiches (& four fags) Jim Berry always jumped on his Bike (that was his transport) & went to Eathorpe to the Plough for a Pint. After we had been working for an hour after lunch Jim would come off the Drum, put his hand on his Tractor & say" she's a boiling & I'm a busting "disappear around a Rick & soon come back smiling! At three o'clock it was more tea (& fags)

When you were threshing beans it was even more of a dusty job as the dust was black! & I soon learnt that they were damned heavy so you didn't fill the bags so much. Beans really were a wretched crop to be involved with but were grown because they were very high in protein (that's why you rarely fed them to horses as it got them "on their toes" & got "itchy legs")

After about four years the Patients stopped coming to farms, so then we had some Displaced Persons (people from Eastern Europe who lost their homes in WW2 when Russia overran their countries) who were living in an old POW Camp at Birdingbury. That's when we first saw Yoghurt & most of us thought Yuk Sour Milk! It was then I saw one of these men pick up a Two & a Quarter Hundredweight bag off the ground in his arms & carry it in front of him, we all thought Wow is that what Yoghurt does for you! He was amazing, if he saw a rat run along the Rick he would grab it & kill it, well I thought I was a bit brave but certainly not like that!

Threshing was one of the hardest sweatiest jobs I think I have ever done but it was luckily only for two or three days at a time. I was always pleased to see Jim Berry, his Tractor, Threshing Drum (with his Bike on the top) & Trusser, going along The Fosse Way.

Bob & Prince

My brother Bob had always been a bit of a "Jack the Lad" & had dabbled in all sorts of deals I suppose it could be called "Ducking & Diving from selling cars to selling plastic Gents Ties & an ingenious Cigarette Lighter that didn't need a spark or petrol, usually at Rugby Market on a Monday (but like a lot of good ideas they disappeared) It was just before the time that Road Transport was Nationalised & Bob started working at Baggington aerodrome (now called Coventry Airport) for a company delivering new cars called Parkers & he lived in a caravan on site. After a while instead of new cars all being driven to dealers, a company called Karrimore? Made articulated units that could carry five at the time on two decks, Bob was soon in his element either driving or mostly fixing them. I know I am biased but he was a genius who really could make anything work. (Except his private life) Alas because there were cars stored in a compound parts were disappearing so it was decided to get a guard dog. Bob found an Alsatian in Nottingham that had been partly train by the Police but didn't finish its training. So it was decided Dad & I would go to Nottingham with him in a van to fetch it. We set off in this Morris Commercial mini bus that was normally used for ferrying delivery drivers, arriving at the farm we were introduced to Prince! Ye G-ds he was nearly the size of a donkey with teeth like a crocodile which he showed regularly as he snarled. Bob seemed to make friends with him & said yes I'll have him, he then said "I'll put two leads on him then Dad & you can hold one each & sit with him in the back". I remember thinking "bugger this I never wanted to work in a circus" & I can honestly say my backside was eating the seat all the way to Coventry especially when Dad decided he wanted a pee & muggins was left on my own but after dad came back Bob decided to take Prince for a pee, why couldn't he do that while I was on my own? Anyway we did get back to Coventry & I have never been more pleased to get out of a van ever. Bob & Prince became best mates, with Bob being able to do anything with him (reckon Prince knew he had met his match) but woe betide anyone else who went in that compound, the thefts not surprisingly stopped immediately. Prince did an amazing job for a number of years but finally succumbed to the Alsatian problem his hind legs gave in & after a lot of heart searching he had to be put down. Bob did get another dog but there was never another Prince! At that time there were many Commercial Vehicle companies around Coventry & Rugby who when they had a problem it was Bob they called, so many makes of Lorries had to have the "Bob touch" & I sometimes spent my "Sundays off" cleaning parts & learning that you always cleaned your spanners after you used them. Also that you use proper spanners as adjustables were Knuckle Busters.

Grandad

Once I reached sixteen I got myself a Driving Licence for a Motor bike & a Tractor though we hadn't got a Tractor for road use, I bought a BSA b8 I think, that was taxed & I insured it (third party only) so Heh I was legal, well almost because I always forgot to put L plates up. It was then I decided to take Dad to see Grandad Goodwin. So on my Sunday off we went, yes I know he shouldn't have been on the back, but he was. We got to Lawford Road & found his house, knocked on the door & a big man opened it, slightly stooped but still imposing. When he saw Dad he at first put his hand out to shake Dad's but then put his arms round him & they hugged each other, not a word was said for a few moments & then Grandad said "You'd better come in" looked at me & said "So you're the young'un are ya" in a deep voice that even at his age put the fear of G-d in you. It was easy to see how Sargent Goodwin would have been able to teach someone to behave themselves! He shuffled a bit as he walked but still looked after himself (with a bit of help from Aubrey's wife (who lived round the corner) & made us a cup of tea. Dad & he did a bit of catching up about his brothers & sister, but there was no mention of Mum, which was very sad after all those years & four kids. It appeared that even though he had been retired from the Police since the thirties he still did detective work for Banks & Hire Purchase Companies checking peoples records through the County Courts before they could get loans. When we left we never thought that this would be the last time we would see him, but he died suddenly shortly afterwards. We did go to his funeral, we all went on the bus, and Mum went as well because she said "at least I will show him respect". I did meet uncle Vernon then but my Aunty from the Channel Islands didn't arrive. What a shame when families fall out, & it has to be a funeral to bring some together. How sad was it that I was the only one of us four who met that Grandad. I don't know whether it was because of the fallout of dad's family but we were never close to Cousins, which as I have got older I regret deeply. Particularly when I hear people talking of First, Second or even further Cousins. But Heh Hoh that's life.

In 1953/4 Dad left "the Lockheed" (I think because his mate from Hunningham who used to give him a lift was moving & he didn't fancy cycling every day) & got a job as Gardener/Handyman at the Hall working for Mrs Twist. It made life shall we say "interesting" because it meant he was paid monthly & a bit less than at the "Lockheed". For someone who was short of money when they were paid weekly being paid monthly was always going to be a disaster! This I'm sure was the final problem with Margaret.

Back to Work

At that time Arthur had two drills for sowing grain, one for Grain (Massey Harris) that was used for Wheat, Barley & Oats, that had a box that held about four bags of seed with a shaft running through which had a series of cogs on that lined up with adjustable slots, that as the shaft turned, driven by the wheels the grain would be pushed through the slot dropping down a flexible tube into the ground that a disc had opened. The other one was a Suffolk Drill still a box but this one had a shaft with wheels fitted with cups that as the shaft turned dipped into the Beans or Mangolds & emptied them down a flexible tube to enter the ground through a wedge shaped Coulter, there were different size wheels for different seeds. It was a very skilled job driving two horses walking behind the wheel that was just across the wheel mark you had just made & also pulling the levers to lower the Coulters & put the shafts in to gear at the end of each bout. If you got it wrong there were gaps to see for the whole of that season. This was particularly important with Mangold & Swede where you blocked every two outlets of the box so you had a gap in-between rows, as they needed room to grow (more about that later)

Arthur usually used those drills & you didn't see gaps he was that good a horseman. Each Drill was about 8ft 6ins wide so could be got through a 10ft gate. He also had a Fertilizer spreader (Nickleson) that again was a box that held about ten bags of Fertilizer. This worked by have slotted plates in the bottom that slid across each other driven by the wheels, to regulate the amount used you adjusted how much the plates moved. Again you walked behind the wheel to follow the last track it was a bit easier with this as you only had one horse to drive! The minus part was even if it was a bit windy you were covered in fertilizer (even when it was granulated) & at that time we used something called "Basic Slag" which was waste from Iron & Steel Works. It was black & was so fine it ran like water (it was in hessian sacks line with cardboard) & was damned heavy. As you walked behind the drill you got covered head to toe worse (I think) than the Coalman. It was used because it worked & was cheap! Corby was not too far away. That was the only time I never went home at lunch time, because your clothes got so full of Basic slag that you had to take them off & give them a good shake before you dare go home & once a day was enough of that. In the Eight years I worked there I think I was the only one to use the Nickleson!

The other drill was a Seed Barrow used for Grass & Clover. It was an A frame with one large wheel at the front & two handles at the back. Again a wooden box with a shaft running through, this time the shaft had brushes fitted which picked up the seed & pushed it through adjustable holes, the shaft was driven by an open link chain from the wheel. There was no horse to pull this, you pushed it! It was a two man job one pushing the barrow & one holding a rope that was half the width of the box & fixed to the end of the box. The man on the rope walked on the last wheel mark & the person pushing had to keep that rope tight, so no ground was missed or over seeded. After an hour you changed jobs! Believe me pushing that Barrow was really hard graft even on the flat, because even balancing an eight foot box was difficult & we were on ploughed land. There was a rope that went from the handles across the back of your neck to tale some of the weight off your arms but when you were pushing my G-d your arms & legs ached. I was always so pleased when that job was done (it makes me realise just how fit we must have been)

The setting of all these Drills for the amount of seed or fertilizer to sow was something you had to learn even though each Drill, had some instructions, there were so many variations of size of seed etc., but Arthur was a genius at setting them up & I did try to learn from him.

Using the Drill for Mangolds & Swedes was even more technical as you had to be accurate to within an inch when driving because the gaps between the rows had to be the same, because as the plants grew so did the weeds between the rows & they had to be removed with a Horse-hoe. This was a tool pulled by one horse that had two wheels at the front A single blade & two horizontal Blades that removed the weeds, the horizontal blades were adjusted so you got as close as you could to the plants without damaging them (to save more work later with a hand Hoe). Again a two man job one leading the horse & the other guiding the Hoe with the handles, again damned hard work on the handles. Arthur always had the handles because he said if he got it wrong & hoed up the plants it was his fault (I believe he thought Ii could do it & he as probably right) & I led the horse, he always used Drummer for this job & Drummer disliked being led by the Bridle so quite often, it was a bit like a Rodeo (again don't know why he used him but he did) The next job with Mangold & swede was singling, which meant you worked along the row & cut out plants to leave only one every six inches, where possible you left a Mangold but if there wasn't one there you left a Swede, you used what was known as the push & pull motion with the Hoe pushing the spare plants forward & then pulling the next backwards & that gave you the six inches spaces between plants. Back breaking work that also gave you blisters on your hands. This was usually done twice, Oh how you looked forward to it. Horse-hoeing was usually done about three times depending on how the weeds grew & the horizontal blades had to be adjusted as the crop grew bigger & Drummer had to be careful not to step on the plants, now that was not always easy if he was in one of his moods!

We didn't use a machine for planting Potatoes. The ground (usually the same field as Mangolds) was ploughed to about seven or eight inches deep and then scuffled, the Ridge plough was then brought out, this was a horse Plough with two Mouldboards & a narrow Share & as it was pulled across the ground (by two horses) made a furrow that as you returned made a Ridge. The Potatoes were the planted in the furrow by hand, you had a sack that you tied a string at each end making a sling in which you put the seed potatoes, carrying the sling so the potatoes in front of you, you then walked along the furrow dropping a seed in front of each step which give a gap of about twelve inches, it sounds awkward but you soon got the hang of it. Once the seed had been planted the plough was used to cover the seed by ploughing the ridges forming new ridges over the seed, again a skilled job driving two horses & guiding the Plough. Arthur always did this & he was brilliant at it even when his back had started to give out. Yes, I did have a go at using this plough to make the first furrows but I was never good enough to risk me near the seed. It was always an education to see him handle horses & keep his pipe alight at the same time I was in awe of that man, because believe me it was not only very skilled work it was also damned hard work. An annual job just before Christmas was catching & killing the Cockerels that Agie had been feeding to fatten, there were always a long list of people ordering her birds. It was always done in the dark when the birds were roosting as they were much easier to catch, me doing the catch & Arthur doing the dispatching. The birds were killed instantly with just a quick twist when I had a go I pulled the poor things head off & there was blood everywhere, not something I was ever good at!

There is more to life than just work

After I left school & before Hunningham School was closed for good, the local Vicar decided to open a Youth Club one evening a week in the School room. Most of us "old Hunningham Pupils" & a few others used to go & play snooker (at which I was rubbish) Table-tennis & generally have a good time. I remember when I found a book that Dad had, it was a plain covered book with spelling mistakes in. Entitled "Lady Chatterley's Lover" (remember this was before it became popular) of course I found the naughty bits! I took it to Youth club one evening after bragging about it for a while. It certainly coursed a lot of interest, so much so that the Vicar wanted to know what it was all about. My G-d I panicked as he took the Book & said "Oh yes, Quite good but a little outspoken in places" I have been embarrassed many times since but NEVER that much. It was decided that a day out on a coach would be a good idea, so we all payed our fare & along with some adults went to Southend to the "Kursall" we had a great time. To me it was like going to some sort of heaven. A lot of my time & money watching & listening to The Wall of Death, I was hooked, so much so I tried hard to get a job with "Tornado Smith" & his show but he wanted someone with good looks & a lot more talent than me. The trip home was something different, with lots of us coupling up, I finished up with Gillian (the one born on the same day as me) which was a bit exciting as her mother was also on the coach, luckily nearer the front & when Gillian fainted there was a bit of a panic (surely nothing to do with what I was doing, I think), Oh happy days & I never knew what happened to that book! But it became legal after a lengthy Court Case sometime afterwards.

Occasionally there would be a new girl working at the Hall as a Nanny or Mother's Help or something like that, which meant us lads had a bit of "fresh talent" (& I'm damn sure they felt the same) anyway we had some fun & a bit of falling out! But the girls never stayed long, don't know whether it was us lads or their employer that had got it wrong.

Having a Motor bike (even an old one) meant that I did get out & about trying my luck with the girls around the area quite often unsuccessfully, but it was fun trying. There was a Coffee bar in one of the Avenues at the top of the Parade at Leamington, & they had a Jukebox! It was there I first heard the Everley Brothers. Some of the Villages we visited were Harbury, Bishops Ichington, Long Ichington, Stretton, & we had great nights at the King's Head at Napton,& the Red Lion at Hellidon, with the Skiffle & Rock & Roll It was here I first heard the record "Heartbreak Hotel by Elvis Presley" but we went there particularly because not only did the Landlord stay open late but had Three Gorgeous Daughters, no good there but I tried, Southam, Daventry & Leamington particularly when they had the Lights in The Jephson Gardens. In 1953 I decided to rent a Television Set, a Twelve inch screen that brought entertainment into our house for Sixteen Shillings a week. We had it in time for the Football Cup final, our house was full with people wanting to watch it most bringing bottles of beer (I think we were about the third to have a tele in Eathorpe) & on the day of the Coronation you could hardly breathe there was so many people. With curtains drawn & me ready to adjust the set if it started to roll or slip sideways & making sure the aerial didn't move it was a sight to behold. I reckon we had more friends then than when we killed a pig! I also got a bit embarrassed by the state of our Sofa & Chairs so I bought some new ones on HP, so with my Keep that I was paying, the Tele & the HP most of my wage was spoken for. But at least Mother could watch the Tele in comfort while Dad was up the Pub & there was always some overtime to boost the wages. One program I loved was "Victory at Sea" that used to be on just before the Tele shut down at 10 30. Having the Tele meant that Oonagh sometimes used to come over & we would have a cuddle on the new Sofa! That Tele did us proud really I think we only had to call the engineer out twice over the years, which was good in those days as you regularly had to adjust the vertical or horizontal hold, & I had many different cuddles on that Sofa.

!952-53 was the year we first heard of" Infantile Paralysis later called Polio, some people in Coventry & surrounding areas were catching this awful thing & having to go into Iron Lungs to breathe. There were people of all ages being paralyzed, it was really scary. It was said it was transmitted by water so some parents wouldn't allow their kids to go near the river, though most of us did & luckily no-one in Eathorpe, Hunningham, Marton Wappenbury, Weston or Princethorpe caught the Virus. When the Salk vaccine came out (which was brilliant) I was too old to need it, but it soon destroyed the virus. Alas it didn't help those whose lives had either been lost or totally changed.

In 1954 I became 18 which meant I had to register for National Service, I went to Leamington & did just that, on going to work the next day Arthur said "did you bring the Deferral Papers?" I replied "no" because I hadn't considered being Deferred (meant you didn't do Service for a given time if you were in certain industries) any way after a lot of discussion I agreed to sign the Papers that Arthur had by then got. And I never did my National Service. That, was one of the decisions in my life that I truly, truly regret as I always fancied the Navy.

Being 18 meant I could legally go in a pub & drink (yes I had been in pubs before but the Landlord of The Plough knew how old we all were & would not allow anyone under age to be in his pub). I started going some nights with my Dad & even joined a Domino team! A drank Ansell's Mild & every night was sick! But still I went. On the first New Year that I was "Legal" my brother Bob came & I went with him & Dad to the Pub & stupidly tried to keep up with him on Gin & Tonic! Bob was an Accomplished Drinker & I got hopelessly Drunk as I finally got into bed the room was not only going round but as I lay my head down it felt as if I was sinking down a well & I had to keep sitting up which made the head ache worse. That was Bloody awful but I still had to be up at 7 O'clock next morning to go to work to feed & tend stock & the have one of Agie's fried breakfasts, I did it but I really thought I was going to die, & from that day for many years never touched booze. How many more times in my life do I have to learn a painful lesson?

When I first left school I embraced the "farming" thing perhaps a bit too much. I bought myself some corduroy riding breeches some rather good (second hand) brown leather leggings & a pair of brown boots. Well, I'd seen some of the old farmers at Kenilworth Show & Rugby Market! I think the important word was old! I thought I looked good but I must have looked like a "Land-girl gone wrong" luckily I soon dropped that "look"

When the Teddy Boy era came along I bought a pair of ordinary black trousers & had them tapered at a Tailors near the top of the Parade (cost as much as the trousers but cheaper than real Drain Pipes) I could never afford a Drape Coat but I did have a string tie! I bought a pair of Brothel Creepers (shoes) with the sponge rubber soles that as you walked on the dance floor you heard a sucking sound & there was the joke that if you stepped in a puddle it dried up, the sole were not unlike the Sorbo? Ones we used to wear a hole in on the front tyre of our bikes. It was at this time we found out that George was carrying a Cut-throat Razor in his pocket when we went out, I'm sure it was just bravado but we all dropped him like a hot potato, country kids we may be but not bloody stupid. It was then I realized that I was never ever going to be a fashion icon, just a country kid.

Back to the Farm

It was about this time Arthur decided to buy another Tractor, the Fordson Standard was traded for an Upright Fordson Major on rubber tyres, not new but in good nick. It was nearly the same engine as the Standard but had a Hand Brake & individual brakes on each wheel & you sat higher up which meant you got colder in the winter because you hadn't got a warm rear axle between your knees. The Majors were built with different ratios at the axle, this one being high & in Third Gear could really shift, too fast for a field & on the road at times the front wheels wobbled so much you had to slow down! At long last I could use my Tractor License. Arthur was having more & more trouble with his back which meant I had to do some of his work. He always hated the Fordson Standard but he even hated the Majors more & I can't remember him ever driving one. A second hand Massey Ferguson Muck Spreader also arrived (one of the best things he ever bought, no more spreading the stuff out of piles on the ground) though it gave me perhaps the biggest scare I have ever had with a tractor. We were spreading muck on some grass fields to give them a lift & to get there had to go down "Rabbit Bury Hill" which was quite steep normally I went down at an angle safely, I don't know whether the grass was a bit wet or I went too straight but the loaded muck spreader overtook me & started to drag the tractor backwards down the hill, with the wheels turning & spinning in opposite directions. I didn't know whether to jump or stay, I stayed & finally the tractor & spreader jack-knifed & a rear wheel jammed on the drawbar, finally stopping a few feet from a big drop. I must admit I was petrified but the only damaged done was a very slightly bent draw-bar, some-one was watching over me that day! I didn't mind the rollicking I got from Arthur, another lesson learnt. Also at this time a big Waggon arrive (I suppose it was a trailer) that Arthur bought at some sale, it had solid rubber tyres & a huge draw bar that could be fitted at either end because all four wheels steered! It was said to have been used behind Steam Engines in WW1, I don't know if that was true but it was damned heavy unladen! It was not long before another Fordson Major arrived & Arthur told me that as Jim Berry was considering retiring & the Horses were getting older, so he had made the decision they were going to go. Perhaps the biggest shock I have ever had.

The End of an Era

Arthur Penteloe was a horse man through & through he grew up with horses on his parent's farm, he went to war with them in WW1 when he was in the Cavalry, enduring the horrors, of losing mates, of living in mud & once, having his horse shot from under him. He was so sure he was not going to survive that, on one leave in Belgium he spent his share of his heritage from his parent's farm. Which meant that when the War was over & he had survived he had nothing, so had to start from scratch. I am sure he never got rich but my wages were always there every week.

Oh My God what a decision that must have been for him! It was not many weeks before a Lorry arrived & Arthur saw his four Horses that he led one at a time from the stable, leave the farm for the last time, we all knew what their fate was & I am prepared to admit there was not a dry eye. I didn't see Arthur for a couple of days, though the other stock had to be tended & we never spoke of Boxer, Jumbo, Beauty or Drummer again. Though I knew Arthur regularly thought of them & at times wished he still had them.

Arthur Penteloe was the last farmer in the area to use mainly Horse Power. No more would there be trips to Marton to the Blacksmiths (though I did go with a tractor & trailer to take some Drag-harrows to have the Tines repointed (quite a long job each tine had to be remove heated & beaten into a point & refitted) & a set of Chain-harrows to have two links remade) No more would we have people stop to take photos, no more would we be fetching in the Horses in the mornings & chasing them round Rabbit Bury Hill when about once a year the buggers didn't want to come in or cleaning out the Stable, no more would we have to hold them by their nose as Arthur filed their teeth sometimes with a twitch or on very wet days would we be oiling Harness to stop the leather cracking, no more would we be walking on ploughed ground or in a Basic Slag Cloud. The Binder, the Hay sweep, Horse hoe & Ridge plough were all put at the back of the shed by the Rick yard. No more would we have Sheaves to Stook, no more Corn or Hay Ricks, no more would we have the gangs for Harvest or Threshing & Hay making was going to be totally different. No more would we grow Mangolds, Swedes, so no more hoeing or when Pulling the Mangold having to cut off the tops & when Pulling Swedes cutting top & bottom usually in the wet trying not to cut off your fingers. No more Ridging Or bending over picking Potatoes or the nightmare of Beans We were still having a change of personnel regularly, this time a young fellow called Chris who I got along with well even though his time keeping was a bit unreliable, I sometimes wondered if it was me!

Going Mechanical

It was 1955 & I was doing the same as all young men do, making silly mistakes but that's part of learning (& I certainly learnt some lessons particularly where the fair sex was concerned. But life at Arthurs was definitely going to be easier but we still had the seed-barrow to push!

Shafts & poles were removed from Waggons, the mower, hay turner, tedder, rake, the flat roller & the corn-drills, so that draw bars, made by the Perce Hands the Blacksmith could be fitted. I had to learn how to reverse a four wheel waggon, a little bit harder than with a horse, but luckily I could do it. We still used the same Plough but because rubber tyres didn't grip in the wet so well as spade lugs we could only plough when ground conditions allowed. So I came up with the idea of making a set of chains just like the ones that were used on cars in snow, but with angle iron bars across the tread. Using old Fore-horse chains & bits of angle iron from I can't remember what, I made them & they worked! Though you couldn't use them all the while as they were liable to damage the tyre but if there was a bit to finish they came in handy & they didn't take too long to fit. I know you could buy Strakes to fit to tractor wheels but Arthur wouldn't buy any. During Corn-drilling Arthur stood on the footboard on the back to work the levers & I drove the Tractor being very careful not to miss the line. He still shouted "Whoa" when he wanted to stop. The Swingletrees were removed from the Harrows & a chain was fixed to the footboard of the Drill so the corn was covered immediately, saving a job. Fertilizer drilling was certainly easier using a tractor but you still got black using Basic Slag. Mowing was certainly different with me driving & Arthur on the Mower as you couldn't reach the lever to lift the knife from the tractor, Arthur regularly yelling either "Whoa or we haven't got any cattle with short necks" if he thought I was going to miss a bit. After one year he decided it was daft having two of us mowing, so instead of buying a tractor mower he got a neighbour to do it with his posh & fast drum mower. Turning, Tedding & rowing the Hay was certainly easier with the tractor even though you had to get off to pull the levers when you needed the lift the tines from the ground (luckily not very often). It then came to the time of using the Massey Harris Baler for the first time, obviously I had had a good look round it (as it was second-hand there was no handbook) I learnt where all the grease points were (very important), the knotter was the same principle as the Binder & Trusser so it was all go! It was not long before I found that being driven by the Power take-off & that was linked to the gearbox that if you put your foot on the clutch the baler would stop even though it had a free wheel device, so I soon learnt just to put the clutch down quick slip it out gear & clutch back up again quick, particularly if you came to a thick bit & I got quite good at that. Occasionally there would be an almighty bang & the shear pin that protected everything had broken usually cause by a broken turner tine or even a stone getting between the ram & the cut-off plate. It was a case of replacing the pin turning the Baler backwards removing the offending article (hoping it hadn't damaged the cutting edges too much) & starting again after reversing a bit to give you a clear start. It was not long before we all found out that if the Hay or Straw was the slightest bit damp the Baler would soon let you know, the bales would get heavier & the crop instead of going from the front elevator to the cross auger would just wrap itself round the top shaft of the elevator & just go round & round, & this took ages & a lot of swearing to cut out. (Another lesson learnt) Picking the bales up & loading them on a waggon (always referred to them as waggons but I suppose they became trailers behind a tractor) was again something to learn, to lift a bale with a fork because they are heavy you should always stick the fork in (obviously) start to lift with one hand on the metal part where the tines are fitted into the handle then put your foot against the handle & lift against your foot till the fork is upright you then lift the bale in the air using both hands, that way you don't break the fork handle in half. Loading the bales you learn the each layer is crossed to hold them together & you get very sore fingers by lifting them by the string. We always had Wilf or Ernie come & help getting the bales in & they were both masters at either pitching bales or building loads or Ricks with them. Most of the Hay bales were put in barns around the farm & in the loft above the stable & a new shelter was built in the Rick-yard for the Baler out of timber with a roof covered with old Basic Slag bags(they worked) there was also room for a lot of bales, so no more Hay-ricks. Harvest time came around & Joe Kenning's brother George, brought their Combine to harvest the crops as they became ready. The Combine was a Massey Harris bagger which meant Arthur rode on the Combine tied up the bags as they filled & slid them down a chute onto the ground then Ernie & I or whoever was available, would go along with a tractor & trailer & using a piece of round wood under one end & holding onto the corner the other end would lift the bags onto the trailer & whoever was stacking the bags on the trailer would take a turn at lifting the bags to give either of us who needed a break. If the corn was to be sold it was left on the trailer, but if it was for feed you had to take it off the waggon on your back & then up those Granary steps! But at least you hadn't got the worry of getting back down before the sack over-filled on the Threshing Drum. Once the bags were cleared I was in with the Baler & there were bales to collect & if they were built in a Rick it didn't have a roof like a Corn Rick just a single row across the middle to keep a Tarpaulin from sagging in the middle & we never had to worry about the Rick getting hot! The next year Kennings had changed their Combine to a Tanker, which meant instead of Arthur riding on the Combine a Grain trailer was borrowed (I think from Kennings) the Combine emptied into that & the grain was bagged up from a chute & then lifted onto the our Trailer, perhaps a little bit easier but not much. Most farmers by now were using Hydraulic mounted machines but we were still behind using the old trailed ones.

Well, that is a surprise

By now it was 1956 & in the spring we had another change of personnel! A lad of 17 or 18 named Bill arrived. His dad worked on a farm on the Long Itchington road & they lived in a house next door to where the Gypsies used to camp. Bill & I got on very well, he didn't pretend to know everything but he was a darned good workmate. Not long after starting work at Arthur's he decided to buy a Motor bike, he bought from a firm who advertised in the Exchange & Mart. The Bike was to be delivered to Marton Railway Station, so I said I would take him on the back of mine to collect it. So off we went with his L plates & a can of petrol. When the train arrived in the Guard's van was this shiny AJS that made mine look really old! After signing the bits of paper, petrol was put in the tank L plates fitted & then after a few kicks away it went. We got back to his house & he was delighted with his pride & joy. We were talking one day & Bill said he would be glad when he had passed his test as he had a Girlfriend from Cubbington & it would be great to be able to take her on the back of his Bike. I never mentioned that I hadn't passed my test though I didn't use L plates but I kept renewing my Provisional License (well at least I had a licence). I had taken a test once & failed it! After he had used the Bike for a few weeks the Primary Chain Case started to leak the mixture of paraffin & oil. As Bill knew absolutely nothing about Bikes,& I'm not sure whether the Bike had to be sent back to the seller or the short warranty had run out, So I said I would have a look (perhaps a bit of bravado as I had never worked on an A J S before). We arranged that I would go on Sunday, I put what tools I had in a bag & also some Gasket Sealer (Red Hermatite). Arriving at Bill's house it was obvious his Girlfriend was there, I was introduced, her name was Noreen & she worked on a farm in Offchurch looking after the Manager's riding Horses. As I was trying to seal this case (always difficult on this model) she started to play with the tools I was using, I suppose she was flirting a bit & I must admit I enjoyed it & perhaps encouraged her even though she was my work mate's girl-friend. (Not the best thing to do but she was good looking). Any way I did seal the case & then it was suggested that I took Noreen home on the back of my Bike & Bill would follow on his because he was on L plates. As we rode along she put her arms round my waist & make no mistake I enjoyed it. When we got to Cubbington Bill & her went for a walk & I went home, (thinking all sorts of things on the way). Quite a few times I took her on the back of my Bike with Bill following on his. I know it sounds strange but that's how it was for a couple or three weeks, until one night I ask her if she would go out with me! She said yes & I gained a girlfriend & lost a mate. Not long afterwards Bill's family moved away & I also lost a workmate even though it became a bit difficult. I know I have said about not stealing, but that wasn't stealing was it? I think it was more like Scrumping with encouragement.

Is she the One?

From that night I went to see her every night come rain or shine & even after working late. We both enjoyed the outdoors. At first accompanied by her friend Sandy! It was not long before Sandy got tired of playing Gooseberry spare part or even perhaps Chaperone. We usually walked along the Offchurch road past Thwaites Engineering workshops that I remember visiting many years before with Chris in an EX WD van when it was just a Blacksmith's Shop to have a fuel tank repaired from a Standard Fordson. We walked arm in arm getting to know each other, it was then I learnt that she had been a good athlete at school particularly at the High Jump & she was most certainly very fit then. One wet evening Noreen suggested I went to her home to meet her Mum & Dad, they lived in a house where I remembered there was a big farm house & yard when I went to Grammar School on the bus. The house & farm belonged to Flannel Reeve's brother who also owned a Corn mill. I must admit I was more than a bit nervous as I had had a couple of run-ins with girl-friend's mums (no, I don't know why). Anyway her Mum & Dad made me very welcome & I started to regularly go in for the obligatory cup of tea (there was always a pot full covered with a cosy). It soon got that if it was wet we stayed in & I think it was about the second evening I met her brother John as he came home from working overtime Ploughing, he worked on a farm on the Fosse Way near Radford Semele that grew potatoes which meant the ground was plough deep using a single furrow plough a very slow laborious job that needed a lot of patience. John was also a Motorbike man but his bikes were much newer & posher than my old EX WD Royal Enfield complete with canvas Saddle Bags. I soon realised that John didn't just have Motor-bikes he had a love affair with them! He looked after them better than some people looked after their children. The Bikes were stored in the covered Entry that was the access to the back door & rear garden of their house. He spent more time polishing them particularly the engines with Auto Solvol (usually in his mum's kitchen)! Than he ever did riding them & if it was raining NEVER took them out. I remember when he went to the Cinema in Leamington, he always paid to park his Bike under cover in the car park of the Regent Hotel, one evening when he came out from watching the film it was raining so he hired a cab home & paid for the bike to stay in the dry overnight, then went by bus to collect it in the morning (it wasn't raining). He had some cracking Bikes, Triumph Tiger 100, Vincent Comet, BSA Gold Star, Sunbeam S8, & a Ducati. He also had a very old AJS that he used for work (Noreen used that for a while for work) John was very Meticulous & whenever he filled up with fuel he would always wipe round the filler after fuelling, he would also carry a notebook & record the mileage & fuel so he knew the MPG & when he did an oil-change it was definitely a major task. John & I soon got on really well & I learnt that Noreen had another brother Colin who was in the Army doing National Service & also a sister Hazel who was at Boarding School near Coventry because she was one of the victims of Polio when she was nine & was paralysed from the waist down. Luckily I soon became part of the family & loved her Mum she was the most incredible cook (my Mum wasn't) & the most genuine lovely person you could ever meet. Her Dad was a Painter & Decorator at Warwick Hospital & was a really generous man who would give you his last penny. He loved going out on his Pushbike collecting watercress in season but he would never let on where it got it from & he knew which wild herbs were of use for all sorts of ills, providing friends with a good supply. He also enjoyed a pint of beer or two at lunchtime at the weekend, which unfortunately didn't suit him & he became argumentative, particularly about politics. But never violent, he was not that sort of man. But he enjoyed the music of Mario Lanza & always played his LP on his radiogram at full whack when he'd had a drink, usually falling asleep before the end. Make no mistake I soon loved them so much I called them Mum & Dad, if we were "staying in" we would all play cards, quite often Brag for penny stakes & if Mum had had a losing evening she always used to say "you'll get thruppence & like it" & we did. Noreen didn't have to work weekends as her Boss looked after his horses then, so she soon started coming with me to Arthur's when it was my weekend on. Arthur & Aggie loved her particularly because she knew a bit about horses & loved animals. I remember twice she came to the farm on one of the horses she was exercising & she looked magnificent on that huge thing, she was certainly a darned good horsewoman & strong enough to stay on board until she could bring it under control when one was spooked & bolted on the road. I also found out that she could whistle using her fingers, well, now there was a bit of male pride going on here. I curled my tongue as she suggested I did everything & still no bloody whistle, G-d was I envious (nearly as much as when I didn't have Dinky toys), it became a running joke about me & not being able to whistle with my fingers. But it all proved that I didn't believe in the old saying that "A whistling girl & a crowing hen are neither use to God nor men" but I'm still not sure about the hen.

It wasn't long before I took Noreen home to meet my Mum & Dad & it went down extremely well with them both but what took Noreen by surprise was our toilet (or lack of) facilities & the fact we didn't have running water. The second time she came to Eathorpe I borrowed a camera from Bob & we walked through the fields to the gated road just like we did when I went to Hunningham School & I took some photos of her with some lambs (after running around to catch them) & I truly think they are the best I have ever taken. I soon bought myself a camera, the first I'd ever owned. During busy times Noreen had to help on the farm as well as looking after the horses. The farm had a pedigree Dairy herd & in late spring a crop of Vetches was harvested for Silage, the crop was cut & the a Green-crop loader was towed behind a trailer & the Vetches were brought onto the trailer where someone had to pull them apart, because as they came up the loader they tangle up & they were not only very difficult to load but would have caused air pockets in the silage pit. I was in between Hay making & Harvest so went along to give a hand (& earn some money) when I found it was Noreen who had the job of loading the trailer while a man drove the tractor, now that I was not amused with. Luckily she was a very strong seventeen year old but when I got on the trailer as well I realised my G-d she needed to be! I was used to hard work but this was evil.

Going to see Noreen every evening & as she didn't swim anyway, I never went in the river again, which I suppose was very sad as it had been such a big thing for me but I really had other things on my mind!

I also bought another Motorbike an elderly Triumph Tiger 70 a 250cc, for Five pounds including a full tank of fuel from Wally Wells at Wappenbury Garage. It was bit nippier than the Royal Enfield, it had a raised exhaust like a scrambler & a dual seat had been fitted, the first time Noreen road pillion she burnt her leg on the exhaust not badly but enough to make sure I made a guard so it didn't happen again, it also developed an oil leak on the rocker feed, actually I didn't know about that until the fine oil spray made holes in her stockings (yes, not tights then) that was soon fixed but what do you expect for a fiver(though that was more than my basic wage for a week & Arthur always said he would retire if he had to pay more than Five pounds a week for basic!) It wasn't long before the big end went, I found the head had been skimmed so much the compression ratio was very high. So it was back to the Enfield until I got the new big end fitted & I rebuilt it. We did many miles on that bike once coming back from a ride on my Sundays off coming through Stratford on Avon after a trip round the Cotswolds the throttle cable broke (the nipple pulled off at the twist grip end) so I road home with my right hand in-between my leg & the fuel tank pulling on the inner cable with Noreen doing the hand signals.

It wasn't long before Hazel came home for Half Term & I actually met her, what an incredible young girl, she was so sparky & didn't believe in "I can't do that" because other than being able to stand & walk there didn't appear that there was anything she couldn't or wouldn't do! Although I did learn she could be a bit of a "madam" if she liked! A good example of her personality was a true story I was told, of her Mum pushing her in her wheelchair in the village & another lady started talking to her Mum over Hazel's head about her. Hazel soon got fed up with that & suddenly said "I may be in a wheelchair & can't walk but I can listen & talk so if you want to know about me, ask me & I will tell you". Obviously her Mum & Dad & particularly John made sure she lived as normal life as possible & also spoilt her a bit (well what else would you expect). I also got to meet Noreen's Grand-parents (her Dad's dad used to play soccer for Aston Villa) & uncles, we used to visit her great aunt Ethel who lived at Harbury & had been the local postwoman (her late husband used to be the local carrier doing delivers with horse & dray), so she knew everyone & they knew her (what a character she was). She always insisted you had a cup of tea(china cups) but the tea was so strong the spoon nearly stood up on its own & you always had to have another one because there was "one in the pot" Your mouth was so dry afterwards your tongue stuck to the roof of your mouth, but we loved Aunt Ethel. On our way home from one visit we called at Chesterton Wind-mill & carved our initials in one of the pillars & I hope they are still there. I remember going to see some of her families friends in a village near Coventry & afterwards they got in touch with her Mum & said" he's very nice but he is not one of us" they thought because I had dark curly hair & because I never wore a shirt at work in the summer I had quite a tan they thought I was foreign!

It was on one of our rides out on the Motorbike I had a real scare, we had been for a ride around Everdon Woods & on the way back at the top of Shuckburgh Hill the police were pulling everyone into the layby. Ye G-ds was I scared! When the two police men got to me they had a look round the old Motorbike & asked us where we had been, luckily not asking to see my license. As we rode away, with me sweating profusely Noreen asked "when did you pass your test"? I tried all sorts of lies but she knew I hadn't. It was not long after scare I did take that dreaded test & passed, Yippee I was now legal!

I must say that all Noreen's family & friends made me very welcome. I did have a bit of a shock when I met Colin & he brought along his girlfriend (from Harbury) Doreen & I realised I knew her quite well from when Fred & I used to go round the village hall dances, but neither she nor I mentioned it, ever.

21 years old

In 1957 I reached the grand old age of 21 & it was decided I as to have a party in the new Village Hall (the first event there) A Barrel of Beer, a few bottles of wine & some lemonade was ordered from the Plough, invites went out to everyone in the village & my mates & family. Come the Saturday of the Party Nina & Jack arrived from Doncaster & family from Stoke on Trent (who painted my canoe) also & they were all staying at our house. Quite a few loaves were cut & slices filled with cheese & ham Margaret had a big cake made, a few bags of Crisps were emptied into bowls & the boxes of glasses collect from the Plough. Ray was asked to play his Accordion for the entertainment (no pay just loads of booze). I collected Noreen & she looked amazing. The party started about 7 30 & it wasn't long before Bob & his lady Ivy, Margaret & Joe along with Arthur & Agie, Mrs Twist, Bert & Rita & all my friends from the area arrived, Choggy even arrived from Stoneliegh, the place was heaving. Everyone wanted to meet Noreen as well as wish me Happy Birthday & as soon as Ray started playing people not only ate & drank (plenty) they sang along or danced. Fred was tucking into the beer & getting really merry & he wasn't on his own, as usual he wanted to dance with anyone. I didn't even have a shandy as I taking Noreen home after the Party but I think Bob had my share. We really did have a great night with everyone happy & no nonsense. Come going home time I know there were some who shouldn't have been driving but there was no Breathalyzer then, Fred had got George on the back of his Bike & perhaps we knew things were not going to be good as he nearly dropped it trying to start it but he insisted he was okay, when they got just before Hunningham Hill cross roads instead of going round a curve he went straight through a hedge between two Poplar trees, luckily not hurting either of them, one foot either way & it would have been very different but his Bike got somewhat bent. It was also decided that Noreen should stay the night, as by the time we had finish packing up & tidying up it was going to be very late, so she slept in the little bed room, Nina & Jack in the other, Mum & Dad in theirs & me & the three from Stoke kipped in the arm chairs & sofa, everyone else went or wobbled home. During the night Noreen needed the loo & as she crept through the bodies in the living room, in bra & pants because she didn't know she was staying! My distant Cousin (who was well & truly drunk) half woke up & in the morning he was in quite a flutter, telling everyone that he had seen a beautiful Angel walk through the room that night. Noreen was a bit embarrassed but I think quite a bit chuffed. I know that lots of people will think that was a rubbish Party, I didn't have or want presents but to me in the 50s it was brilliant, because it was the first Birthday party I had ever had. We didn't know then but it was to be the last time our family would ever be able to have such a "do".

Fags

I grew up with the smell of tobacco smoke, Dad smoked, Mum did occasionally, Bob & Nina did but I don't remember Margaret ever partaking, so it was really no surprise that after trying it out early on with the thin fags we made, as soon as I was legal (sixteen) I openly smoked, never more than twenty a day & the cheapest I could buy, because I really couldn't afford to. In those days smoking was not only acceptable but encouraged by adverts etc. Dad had the "smokers cough" in the morning & used to say "bloody coffin nails" but still puffed away, with two fingers on his right hand brown with nicotine. Mrs Rance used to keep her cigarette in her mouth & had an orange stripe in her hair. Noreen also smoked, her dad used to roll his own fags using a dark Shag & never threw a dog-end away, just adding to his supply in his tin, I tried one or two of these but they nearly blew your head off & your throat felt like you had been swallowing razor blades. Her Mum never smoked & John always wanted to, so he could be "part of the crowd" but couldn't get on with it. Arthur always had his trusty pipe & Aggie smoked Craven A, she also had an orange streak in her hair. (Arthur had Groceries, Whiskey Tobacco & Fags Craven a delivered every fortnight by Burgess of Royal Leamington Spa, but quite often would run short of Tobacco, so I would be sent on his little James Motorbike to collect more, it was a mixture of a Flake of which I've forgotten the name & thick Twist. That was a volatile mixture that sent clouds in the sky that could be seen from a distance).

Noreen & I started going to the Cinema on Friday nights & would call at a Tobacconist's on the Parade & buy perhaps some coloured Cocktail Cigarettes or some thin extra-long ones or even a pack of Camel(didn't like those much) to smoke while watching the film. If it was my weekend off I would stay at Noreen's house after the Cinema, sleeping with John as there was three bed rooms, but that was OK. And it meant I could have a proper bath, in fact I used to have so many baths there I used to give her Mum a bit towards the Electricity. Alas Noreen's Dad's smokers cough got so bad he would have bad coughing fits & turn blue but like us all carried on.

Yes she is the One, but an awful year for the Goodwins

Just before May 28th 1958 I asked Noreen's Mum & Dad if we could get engaged after asking her of course & they all said yes. So it meant a trip to Coventry to choice the Ring, one we both liked & could afford. Well that was the plan but Noreen decided that I should also have a Ring, so that day we bought two. I was so proud when we showed off our rings (even though they had very small diamonds in them)

As Noreen had never seen the sea I decided to take her to Mablethorpe (just about the closest seaside) after asking her Mum & Dad because we were going to stay overnight, on a Saturday we set off on the Triumph. We arrived at the seaside & she loved it even though the tide was out! We then looked for a B&B that wasn't too expensive, finding a nice little bungalow place we booked in as Mr & Mrs Goodwin (different days then) & she turned her Engagement ring round so it looked like a Wedding ring.

This was going to be the first time we had actually slept together, yes we had been making love for some time but always with protection (I didn't have to go to the Barbers as Oonagh's Boy-friend was a Hairdresser & he kept me supplied). After a stroll in the evening we went to bed & I realised I had forgotten to put the "Packet of Three" in my pocket & as I couldn't be sure of myself behaving I slept in a tight pair of swimming shorts, (no Morning after Pill then). Next morning we went for breakfast & the ring was turned! It was the first time either of us had ever had a meal at a B&B or a Hotel! After another look at the sea & a walk on the sand, it was homeward bound with Noreen perhaps cuddling even a bit tighter.

About two weeks after this Mum was having more problems with her nerves, so called the Doctor he came & checked her over, Dad came home from work at the Hall & said to the Doctor "I don't know what's wrong with my arm but I'm having a job to use it" the Doctor looked at it a said "a bit of rheumatism I think". The next morning I went to work as usual but when I came home for lunch Dad was sat slumped in his chair lop sided & unable to speak, Mum had been to the telephone box & called the Doctor & was waiting for him. When the Doctor arrived he said he had had a major Stroke, but because it had happened some hours before there was no point sending him to hospital. I was so pleased Noreen saw Dad before that day because he was never the same again. He never regained the use of his right arm, his right leg dragged & his face was always down on the right side, he did regain his speech but his temperament changed completely. He went from being a bit laid back really to being the most cantankerous person ever (I know he couldn't help it but it made life very difficult) the only treatment he ever had was he was given a rubber ball to try & squeeze to make his hand work.

He bought a green-house to try & grow things Also tried drawing again (he used to be quite an artist if he could be bothered) but everything he drew was lopsided & he got so angry.

From that day dad & I never "got on" I don't know whether it was me or him but I lost my mate & found someone who was very difficult to get along with. I found myself spending more & more of my time at Noreen's home. The only good thing that came out of those Strokes (yes he had more) was that

Margaret put the wars that had gone on between them & started to visit regularly & was a brilliant support. I don't know how but she seemed to be able to get through to Dad better than anyone which was surprising considering their history.

Nina came down from Doncaster to see what she could do but she didn't have the same effect as Margaret even though fair dues she tried her hardest. It was obviously awful for Mum but amazingly she coped with his moods & having to dress him etc. extremely well considering she had problems of her own. For years Mum had suffered with her nerves (Dad always used to say "She was alright till she had you & they gave her a Hysterectomy". I once saw her stomach & the operation scar was horrendous, I'm sure the butcher who killed our pigs could have done better). In those days only Barbiturates or Shock Treatment was available. Oh well something else I was not too good at, being born!

That's an Old Man's tool!

By now the old Triumph's big end was starting to knock again so I decided to look for something else & Noreen's neighbour had a Triumph 500 & Side-car for sale. It looked pretty smart & ran well, after a chat with Noreen I forked out the twenty five pounds & it was mine (the most I'd ever spent on a bike) It meant that Noreen didn't get wet in the rain & her stockings didn't get ruined by engine oil! OK I missed her arms round my waist but you can't have everything. One of my Mates after he saw me on the on the Bike & sidecar said "bloody hell Gudgeon that's an Old Man's tool" but I was an "old Man" of nearly twenty two! Having the Sidecar meant I could collect Hazel from school at home weekends or holidays, it certainly caused a stir the first time I arrive to pick her up. With me lifting her out of her wheelchair putting her in the Sidecar & squeezing her wheelchair in too. They did get used to me as I did it quite a few times, sometimes with Noreen on the back if she was not working overtime to earn extra money for us, which meant I got the cuddle again.

That Bike was definitely the most reliable I ever had.

I sold the 250 Triumph to one of John's friends who was into Bike Sprinting. After stripping it rebuilding & setting it up to run on Methanol it was ready for the first Sprint. As the flag went down he open the throttle, there was an almighty Bang & the engine flew in bits. So that was RIP that bike.

Time to save

We immediately started to save for our home, the Cinema & the fancy fags were out. Noreen decided that she could earn more money working at Flavel's a factory making Gas Cookers even though she was going to miss those horses & by working damned hard there earned more than I did each week. By then the tele that I had been renting had got so old the company said "it's yours" & I had payed for the Three Piece Suite so I had money to save, we allowed ourselves just enough for fags & fuel after paying our board, & the rest went into a tin. We spent many Saturday mornings in Baileys on Warwick Street looking at furniture & working out what we thought our home would be like & what we could afford.

Very Big decisions to be made

Obviously started to consider where we wanted to live, when I told Arthur about us getting engaged, he said "well you know that there is my cottage for you" (the one two doors from Mum & Dad).

That was always going to be a problem. Firstly I didn't want to start married life in a house without running water etc even though I was used to it. But the main reason that I was sure it would not be right living that close was (I suppose I was being selfish) I didn't think it would be right expecting Noreen to have to be "nurse maid "to Mum & Dad. As I just knew it would not work for any of us. Even though it was going to mean that I was going to leave the place I grew up in & loved.

It was very, very difficult having to leave Arthur Penteloe's because he had always kind of treated me like the son he never had, but we all have to make those sort of decisions in life, don't we?

After asking Noreen's Mum & Dad we fixed the date of the wedding for 28th March Easter Saturday 1959 at Cubbington Church, with John as Best Man & Hazel & Barbara (Nina's Daughter) as Bridesmaids & a bit of a "do" in Cubbington Village Hall. As usual there were the discussions about who would be invited etc. as there always is, with the usual niggles here & there but nothing too drastic though my Mum did try a bit.

I then had to tell Arthur I was leaving & the next time he saw Noreen he said "I knew I should have shot you the first time I saw you" jokingly. But he wished us well wherever we went as he knew what the situation was. I then bought the Farmers Weekly every week looking for jobs that caught my eye & applied for a few. But after going for some interviews & finding that, for instance one place your wife was expected to work at "the Big House" when they had parties or I was expected to work in the garden at times etc. there were some that I turned down. There were also some that after checking I didn't even apply but there was one we both thought looked good & that was in Northamptonshire.,

After checking on a map where Bugbrooke was. I rang the number & got an interview after giving Arthurs number for a reference.

So on a Saturday we travelled to Bugbrooke past Daventry where Fred & I had some "interesting" times, through Weedon & by where they were just starting work on the M1. We arrived at Bugbrooke after what seemed ages & found this big yard with a huge new building (which I later found was a grain store & dryer) a big Tithe Barn & a Beautiful house. With some trepidation we knocked on the door to be met by a tall man who spoke quite posh (like I was expected to speak at the College) Mr Radburn Adams.

We were invited in & introduced to Mrs Adams (who spoke even posher) & the eldest son Mike, we learnt there were three sons & a daughter. We were told about the farm, it was about 600 acres, had a Dairy herd (no, no more milking as there was a cow man), a flock of sheep with shepherd, store cattle at a Farm at the next village that were looked after by a stockman / general farmworker & grew a lot of corn. There were three Tractors, a David Brown 20D, a Ford Super Major & an old Minneapolis Moline from the WW2 that was only used for driving a corn-mill at the Dairy Farm, there was a Massey Harris Combine & a Massey Baler with a Standard Vanguard engine.

Obviously I was asked what I could do & I told them all I had learnt, being careful not to mention that I had never used a diesel tractor with hydraulics but I knew I would soon work round that as I had seen John ploughing with a Super Major & hydraulic plough. We talked money & the wage offered was very good. We then went to look at the cottage that went with the job. It was in a row of four built of Northamptonshire stone on the village High Street opposite a pub! It had a kitchen, dining room & a sitting room two bedrooms & an upstairs bathroom, with hot water from an electric immersion heater. That meant running water, flush toilets electricity, gas & hot water, my G-d it was an old property but like a new world.

There was also an outside toilet & shed in the communal yard. The other three cottages were all occupied by members of one family, the Cow man lived in the end, his daughter & husband lived in the next, then the one we were offered & then the Cow man's sister & mother the other side.

Anyway I was offered the job & was given a week to think about it. It didn't seen half as far home (it never does). That evening we spent a lot of time talking to Noreen's Mum & Dad about what we had seen & been offered & they were fully supportive of whatever we decided. I told my Mum & Dad about it & they were not particularly pleased about me moving away. Margaret even though it would mean she would have to do more thought it was a great idea to give us space to start our life together. So after a couple of days we decided yes we were going to Bugbrooke & I phoned Mr Adams to say yes I would take the job & be starting in eight weeks' time.

We spent even more times at Baileys buying stuff, I remember once we were going to buy a Kitchen cupboard & table but they hadn't got what we wanted & had to order it but as we had money in our hand we bought a tumble Drier instead! Wow a Tumble Drier it was the first I'd ever seen. The next week the kitchen cupboard & table, which actually was not just a Kitchen cupboard but had a good size Formica topped table that pulled out in two sections on wheels, as in stock, so we bought it. All the furniture including a very futuristic (at that time) three piece suite & matching sideboard, dining table & chairs etc. were all stored at Baileys waiting to be delivered wherever & whenever we wanted them. I can't remember why but I had a bed & mattress delivered to Eathorpe & Mike Adams came in the farm EX Army Hillman Van & collected it for us, as they would fit on a Motor bike & sidecar!

The Church was booked (we had to pay extra because the Church had been decorated with flowers for Easter), the Village Hall was booked & Noreen's parents said they would provide a buffet spread. The Bridesmaids Pink dresses were made & Noreen borrowed a beautiful Wedding dress from their neighbour that fitted beautifully, John & I decided we would wear Beige cord Jackets & trousers to match. Only one Ring was bought this time. We decided that I didn't need a Stag Night & Hen Nights were not that usual then & we couldn't afford them.

Noreen was earning quite a bit more than me so we were being able to buy things. We were visiting Bugbrooke when we could taking stuff over that we had acquired, one evening we loaded the sidecar & Noreen was going to follow on the back of John's Bike so he could see our cottage. I went ahead because John could go much faster than me, I went through Staverton (another old stomping ground) & just as I was nearing Daventry the Bike didn't seem right & I soon realised I had a puncture in my front tyre. I knew there were no garages around there but I decided to push the Bike & loaded sidecar to Daventry, after trying me soon found you can't push a bike & sidecar with a flat front tyre, the only way you can move it is by pulling on the front forks. By now it was getting dusk & drizzling I thought "John & Noreen will be along soon" & as I was pulling the damn thing nearer Daventry I heard John's Bike, then in a flash they were past me & disappearing. I thought they were joking & would turn back, they weren't & didn't. After an awful lot of sweating & swearing I got near a little local shop & asked if they had any idea where I could get the puncture repaired. The bloke behind the counter (who luckily was a biker) said "mate the only thing I reckon is, I will shut the shop you stay with your bike & I will go to Braunston as there's a bloke there who keeps bike spares, I'll get a new inner tube & then I'll help you fix it I've got a foot pump". Now I didn't know that bloke from Adam but that is exactly what he did & his wife even made me a cup of tea, they were certainly guardian angels to me that night & I will never forget them. After well over two hours I arrived at Bugbrooke to be greeted with "where have you been we have been worried about you" After hearing my tale of woe it seemed that as it was drizzling John didn't see me because his glasses had got rain on them & Noreen was tucked right up to him. I had never ever felt that knackered (even when Threshing) or alone as I did at that time. We soon unloaded the sidecar & made our way back to Cubbington. Even though it was really late when we got back (John stayed at my speed home, which went against the grain) Noreen's Mum had stayed up & there was that cup of tea & a homemade cake for us. It was unusual for her to stay up & quite often after her Mum & Dad had gone to bed things got a bit steamy & the moment quite often interrupted by a voice from the top of the stairs saying "Noreen aren't you coming to bed tonight" she knew what the score was. I had for quite a while called them Mum & Dad & they treated me brilliantly. I only once had a fall out with Noreen's Dad & that was on a

Sunday when he had been to the Club at lunchtime, he put his usual Mario Lanza LP on the radiogram & Noreen asked him to turn it down a bit. He then started shouting at her saying that "the only ones in the family were those that had been away" (Hazel & Colin). Well I took umbrage as I knew John & Noreen had done their bit for the family. Luckily he soon fell asleep so no harm was done & I was very pleased because, I know if I had done what I felt like doing I would have regretted it & we didn't mention it again. I never ever had a cross word with her Mum she was incredible, she was definitely not a well woman & spent a fair amount of time in hospital but her spirit was uncrushable & she only ever saw the good in people. I got to love her perhaps more than my own Mum (which is not good I suppose but it happened to be true). John was certainly in a way like the brother I never had! With Bob being that much older & being away so much (in the Army as I grew up)

Wedding Day 28th March 1959

The Big day arrived, the food was taken to the Village Hall. Wally Wells's wife was bringing Mum & Dad, Barbara (Bridesmaid) Nina & Jack in her big car & she was also going to take photos. Noreen & Hazel went next door to get ready & dressed so I couldn't see her before in Church. I got changed at Noreen's house at least two hours early feeling really nervous but not as bad as her Dad but he didn't have a drink to steady his nerves as I think he would never have let his daughter down & her Mum had laid down the law. John & I made our way to the Church which was looking lovely with the Easter flowers Noreen's Mum came with the Neighbours in their car. Hazel & Barbara were brought to Church by Noreen's Uncle Bill. Mrs Wells after dropping off my Mum, Dad Nina & Jack, collected Noreen & her Dad. There were so many people outside the Church it was amazing, which made me even more jittery. As we waited John checked he had the Ring a dozen times & she was late! From all accounts Mrs Wells said "let him wait" & drove round Cubbington twice.

As the organ struck up the Wedding March & Noreen & her Dad walked up the Aisle I could have easily burst into tears as she looked absolutely gorgeous in that white dress with her Dad proudly holding her arm & the two Bridesmaids following behind. Neither of us forgot our vows & the service went very smoothly. I must admit when I put the Ring on her finger I was extremely proud. After signing the register we went outside for photos & there were even more people watching Wow.

After what seemed ages the photos were done & we were then driven to the Village Hall in the car with ribbons on for the reception.

A lot of work had been put into setting everything up & it looked great. It was so good to see so many of our families, (though it was so sad to see my Dad so ill he obviously wasn't enjoying the day) Bob & Ivy, Margaret & Joe, Nina & Jack, Colin & Doreen, Noreen's Uncle & gran parents & of course friends & neighbours. The spread was superb & the Cake looked & tasted delicious. We didn't do speeches but I just thanked everyone for the presents we had been given & to both our parents for all they had done for us. After most of the food was eaten & the conversations were getting shorter. Noreen & I said our farewells to everyone & went to her house to get changed ready to load all the presents & get on the Bike & sidecar to travel to Northamptonshire, it was only 26miles but that day it could have been the other side of the world, as we travelled to start our new life, still in a village but Oh so different. We were so grateful for all that had been done for us particularly by Noreen's Mum & Dad my new in-laws & we knew that everything would be tidied etc for us by family & friends & we looked forward to seeing The Photos.

Farewell Eathorpe

Wow what a day! We became husband & wife starting a new adventure but to do that I finally had to say farewell to Eathorpe, the Village & the Community I had been privileged to grow up in, with the sort of friends anyone would wish for & be proud of. Of course I went back to Eathorpe many times as Mum & Dad lived there till 1974 & Margaret lived up the hill at Wappenbury Hall Farm but I could no longer say I lived in "Eathorpe that Village (Hamlet) on the Fosse Way"

I Know some people thought I was a disappointment as I never went to University like a lot of my peers at "the College", but I consider I DID go to a university "The University of Hard Graft & Knocks" where there were no excuses for not doing something the right way, OK you don't have a Graduation Ceremony or Certificates but I have always had money in my pocket & food in my belly, sometime too much of the latter but not too much of the former but I've down OK. I am so pleased I was born before the "I'm entitled to generation" I was taught you are only given two things in life, one is life & the other is your name. The rest including Love you have to work for.

I will always be grateful to everyone in & around Eathorpe for teaching me all the things you can only learn by actually doing them in the proper country way, those things I needed &

believe it or not there are so many, that I like to think have made me the person I am & yes always have been proud to say I'm

Just a Country Kid

I hope you enjoy growing up with me in the "Wilds" of Warwickshire 1936/59